Studies in
Kant's Aesthetics

for Kurt von Raumer

Studies in
Kant's Aesthetics

EVA SCHAPER

*for the Edinburgh
University
Press*

© Eva Schaper 1979
Edinburgh University Press
22 George Square, Edinburgh

ISBN 0 85224 359 6

Set in Monotype Plantin by
Speedspools, Edinburgh and
printed in Great Britain by
The Scolar Press Ltd
Ilkley, Yorks

Preface

These studies have grown out of a long-standing interest in Kant's philosophy as a whole and a preoccupation in particular with his aesthetic thought. With the exception of chapter 2 they are based on previously published material that has in various degrees been revised or altered for this volume.

Kant's theory of aesthetic judgement cannot, I suggest, be understood in isolation from the rest of his Critical philosophy. Rather than attempt a systematic presentation of that theory, however, I identify some of its central themes and discuss them in terms relevant to contemporary aesthetic inquiry. Since the issues with which I deal are essentially interconnected, there is a certain amount of overlap between the chapters, but not, I hope, much repetition. Discussion in some might even serve to supplement a rather cursory coverage of the same ground in others. All reflect a concern with the role of imagination in its relation to thought and perception, although only chapter 1 is explicitly about imagination and knowledge. Chapter 2, 'Epistemological Claims and Judgements of Taste', and chapter 3, 'Aesthetic Appraisals', explore the contrast between subjective and objective validity of judgements, and examine knowledge claims *vis-à-vis* aesthetic assessments. In chapter 4, 'Free and Dependent Beauty', I try to throw light on a particularly complicated Kantian distinction which, considering its relevance to the claims of formalists and their opponents alike in art theory, has so far not received the detailed attention it deserves. Chapter 5, 'Schiller's Kant', tells a story of influence and creative distortion. Chapter 6, 'The "As-If" Element in Aesthetic Thought', argues that the relationship between the aesthetic and the non-aesthetic is best approached by way of the notion of 'aesthetic transposition'. Kant's characteristic mode of reasoning, the transcendental method, is prominent throughout, as is my conviction that the logical implications of his theory can be exhibited without reliance on an outmoded doctrine of mental faculties that is apt to obscure the scope and value of his contribution.

One of the more agreeable results of preparing this book for publication has been the discovery of the consistency, even after several changes of mind on points of detail, of my view of Kant – a discovery all the more agreeable for being unexpected. I have not included anything that I now think is radically mistaken, but I certainly would not claim that the problems I deal with have been finally solved. A great deal still remains to be done, for this is a field of Kant studies that is relatively unexplored, especially by philosophers in the analytic tradition. A noteworthy exception is D.W. Crawford, whose *Kant's Aesthetic Theory* (University of Wisconsin Press 1974) came to my notice too late for me to record here my assessment of its argument. One of my hopes is that the present volume might persuade at least some philosophers that the problems of aesthetics are as intricate and rewarding as any in the philosophy of mind or epistemology and Kant's philosophy more than a chapter in the history of ideas.

Any shortcomings of this book are entirely mine; where arguments are sound, they may not always be entirely mine – for while long, my struggle with Kant has not been solitary. Terry Greenwood of Glasgow University has become involved in it, and I owe more to his incisive criticism and his knowledge of Kant than he is willing to admit. I also wish to thank Professor W. H. Walsh who has encouraged me to persevere with this project and made valuable suggestions. Dr Betty Redfern has read more drafts than she can have foreseen when she first offered to act as a sounding board for matters of style and composition, and I am very grateful for her meticulous attention to detail and generous sacrifice of her time. Anne Valentine, Wilma White and Sylvia Brown between them have typed with great efficiency and patience through the draft stages to the final version. My thanks are also due to the Publications Board of the University of Glasgow and the Carnegie Trust for the Universities of Scotland for their help towards publication.

EVA SCHAPER
Glasgow, November 1978

Contents

Note on References

Quotations from Kant's *Critique of Pure Reason*
are identified by the Berlin Academy page references,
first and second editions denoted by A and B respectively.
The English translations used are by Norman Kemp Smith
(London : Macmillan 1933).

Quotations from Kant's *Critique of Judgement*
are identified by section (§) numbers and Berlin Academy
page references. The English translations used are by
J. C. Meredith (Oxford : Clarendon Press 1911 and 1929).

Quotations from Kant's
Prolegomena to any Future Metaphysics
that will be able to present itself as a science
are identified by section (§) numbers.
The English translations used are by Peter G. Lucas
(Manchester : Manchester University Press 1953).

Imagination and Knowledge

Kant's doctrine of imagination seems well enough known; but
what exactly is it? Despite the range and variety of critical and
expository work being done on Kant we are still far from having
a coherent, intelligible picture of his views on imagination. We
are even further from a considered assessment of Kant's contribution to the elucidation and resolution of those problems
involving the concept of imagination that now exercise philosophers.

Let me say at once that I am not in a position to supply such
a picture or such an assessment. For one thing, the subject is too
large; for another, there are some central but baffling elements
in Kant's arguments that I have not so far been able satisfactorily
to sort out. Nevertheless, I am fairly clear about what Kant is
not saying; or, if he sometimes appears to be saying it, cannot
have meant; or, if sometimes meant, ought not to be taken
seriously in view of his general aims. So part of what I have to
say will be negative and polemical, concerned with a number of
views that either cannot be right, or are seriously misleading, or
are so oddly slanted as to obscure what may turn out to be of
more lasting significance. What I have to put in their place is, on
this occasion, no more than a sketch of country still to be fully
explored.

The obvious place to look for Kant's considered views on
imagination would seem to be the third Critique. But the
Critique of Judgement is hardly a model of clarity and consistency.
Besides, it presupposes the other two Critiques in more than a
trivially chronological sense. This holds for the general structure
of its argument as well as for Kant's doctrine of imagination,
which forms an integral part of it. Without a full inquiry into the
Critique of Aesthetic Judgement, a discussion of this doctrine

is, of course, incomplete. Yet it would be rash to embark on this before some more general questions on imagination have been sorted out. These arise mainly from the *Critique of Pure Reason* and are of a logical rather than a purely exegetical nature.

(I)

In philosophers' accounts of the nature of our experience of the world, imagination is often assigned a role more or less remote from our ordinary conceptions of this phenomenon. Best known in this respect is the psychological empiricism of David Hume, in which imagination appears ubiquitously as part of the account of how we come to believe many things for which we have no rational justification.[1] In particular, imagination is thought by Hume to be instrumental in the formation of our idea of the continued and independent existence of objects of which we have no present experience, an idea that Hume finds rationally indefensible. This rather specialised use of the concept of imagination as that which connects or unites discrete impressions of sense is concerned with the origin and justification of our ideas of identity, and with recognition of the identity of material things through time. Now in so far as Kant employs the notion of imagination in the solution of just such problems as Hume raises here with respect to our experience of an objective world, it may seem that Kant's view of the nature and role of imagination in experience is something of an embarrassment. For if it is Kant's main task in the *Critique of Pure Reason* to adduce the necessary presuppositions of experience – and it is the carrying out of this task that represents Kant's most notable achievement over and against empiricist philosophies of experience – his use of the notion of imagination seems both essential to establishing such presuppositions and to represent no advance at all on the unsatisfactory account of Hume. We need only think of the well-known passage in which Kant speaks of the power of imagination as a 'blind but indispensable function of the soul, without which we should have no knowledge whatsoever, but of which we are scarcely ever conscious' (A 78). This seems not so much a characterisation of the concept of imagination as a confession that Kant has no analysis to offer.

But too pessimistic a conclusion would be as premature as

making the above quotation central to Kant's account. Let us first consider some invitations that are so easily read into the Critiques – invitations to indulge in speculative metaphysics; or to delve into the murkier areas of equally speculative psychology; or even to weld these two improbable regions together in some species of transcendental philosophy. To accept any one of them is to adopt an approach to Kant on imagination that does not stand up to scrutiny. All three invitations ought to be declined.

The first view, the metaphysical interpretation, has the broadest sweep. According to it imagination is in some way the basis of aesthetic and teleological judgements, and these bridge the gulf between nature and morality. Imagination, then, provides a link between knowledge and freedom. Kant's epistemology and Kant's ethics become reconciled in his teleology which affords access to the supersensible.

The second view, the psychological interpretation, takes the *Critique of Pure Reason* to be presenting a doctrine of faculties that compartmentalises all human mental capacities. Imagination, then, is a faculty operating somewhere between sense and understanding, a third power with connections in both camps, combining the intuitional character of sense with the spontaneity of intellect whilst yet not being co-extensive with either or both of these two basic faculties.

The third view, obscurely aware of the transcendental nature of Kant's arguments, yet feeling strongly the pull of the psychological interpretation, contrasts the empirical employment of imagination with its transcendental employment, and regards Kant as fumbling in the first Critique towards this distinction, which only fully emerges in the third. I shall refer to this view – not very felicitously, I am afraid – as the dualist interpretation.

All these views can claim some support from the Kantian text. But taken individually or jointly they attribute to Kant oddly incoherent views. And the views on imagination which emerge from them are singularly unmemorable. Imagination, it seems, has a function that is hardly comprehensible apart from the Kantian system. It is the function of a kind of glue, joining everything disparate, bridging gaps, and scaling the whole off against any attempt to understand it from outside. Only by our being in the system, by speaking its language, can Kant's doctrine of imagination then be expounded. It does not seem possible to apply what Kant says to the problems *we* might wish to raise, for example problems about the nature of imagination and its objects, and the criteria by which we might distinguish imagined content from perceptual content, and so on. This is, of course, not yet to say that any of these views are mistaken; but it should make us wonder whether Kant could not do better than that.

The first view, the metaphysical interpretation, holding that imagination is the key to overcoming otherwise irreconcilable opposites, contains a prior commitment to the view that there is indeed a conflict or disparity to be overcome between nature and freedom, science and morality, phenomena and things-in-themselves. This is to adopt a position with respect to our thought about the world and about man's actions that is at variance with Kant's critical inquiries into the logical presuppositions and conceptual frameworks of empirical knowledge and of moral agency. On the one hand we have arguments for the necessary conditions and limitations of knowing and of describing what we can know in a space-time world of things and events; on the other we have arguments for the conditions under which it makes sense to say that persons act freely and are morally responsible for their actions. If a gap exists between the realm of nature and that of freedom, this can only be a picturesque way of pointing to the very different kinds of conceptual presuppositions involved in each inquiry. Moreover, if we are puzzled as to how the conceptual presuppositions of the one inquiry could fit into a unified scheme that includes the other, as we might be, *this* puzzlement is not one that any supposed gap-bridging capacity of the imagination could solve. For if we are now thinking of the role of imagination in Kant's account of aesthetic and teleological judgements, the sense in which such judgements occupy, so to speak, the intermediate ground between judgements of the two other kinds can only be that of indicating those peculiar logical features of aesthetic judgements that seem to pull us now in one direction, now in the other, and which it is the business of a Critique, the third in this case, to clarify. Results gained in such an inquiry, however, will not, and cannot, supply answers to the questions that the metaphysical account of the gap between nature and morality poses. What is more, the gap theory prejudges our thinking about the world and human action in a way that is not even clearly and unambiguously Kant's. Certainly many believe that it is; but if they are right, some of Kant's most remarkable achievements would seem to be put in question.

The psychological interpretation is at once both easier and harder to challenge. Easier, because we are in any case accustomed now to reading eighteenth-century philosophy with a finer logical ear for the implications of its psychologising language; harder, because, however finely attuned our ears, there is so much in Kant's references to imagination that seems never to get beyond crude aprioristic psychological theory. This seems, *prima facie*, to be especially true of his apparatus of mental powers and capacities, amongst which it is customary to include *Einbildungskraft* as a faculty functioning alongside sensibility and understanding as they appear in the Transcendental Aesthetic and Analytic of the first Critique. A faculty of imagination is required, on this view, to operate in harness with the faculties of sense and of understanding in the general account of how the mind subsumes items of experience under concepts and recognises some of them as experiences of the same object. Thus, it is claimed, the otherwise enigmatic Schematism chapter is clear in at least one respect: schemata are 'products of the imagination', and they enable us to apply concepts of the understanding to what is given in sense.

There is an aspect of this view that must strike us as open to immediate objection. If we do assume a doctrine of faculties, a hypostatisation of our mental powers, the most that Kant's arguments explicitly allow for is the trinity of sense, understanding and reason. No room is left for an extra faculty of imagination, and Kant is clear on this point: he repeatedly asserts that the tripartite scheme is complete. If we adopt a straightforward reading of the faculty doctrine we cannot have it both ways, that is accept sense, understanding and reason as exhausting the capacities for coping with experience, and then demand that only with the aid of imagination, another faculty, does the whole mechanism work. If we do not insist on a rigid scheme of faculties, however, Kant's apparently ambivalent attitude towards the status of imagination can find some sort of explanation in the place this notion has in the structure of transcendental arguments concerning experience of an objective world. This point will be taken up in section 11.

There is, in any case, no reason why we should insist on the faculty doctrine. The idea that when it comes to imagination we are dealing with a 'faculty' can arise from a too literal translation of *Einbildungskraft* as 'power of imagination' – a phrase that seems almost to have built into it the suggestion of an agency of the mind. Yet no special importance attaches to 'power of' in a translation of *Einbildungskraft*, any more than it does to 'power of' in a translation of *Urteilskraft* as the title of the third Critique. We speak of the *Critique of Judgement*, for it is judgement that is at stake and not any particular power or special faculty for making judgements. However, given the sense of 'imagination' with which we are concerned, to use the German word *Einbildung* without the *-kraft* would invite confusion with a sense of imagination that is not up for discussion in the central passages of the Critique, namely that which suggests delusion, or mere imagining or fancy.

With the psychological reading of Kant thus put in question, it will already be clear why the third approach, the dualist approach, will also have to be discounted. For it does take the psychological view for granted in what Kant says on imagination in the first Critique, but maintains that the third Critique makes good the earlier work's shortcomings. According to this view Kant comes to see that no merely empirical employment of the imagination as binding experiences together could form part of the ground for the possibility of empirical judgements. From this the somewhat strange conclusion is drawn that a 'transcendental power' of imagination is essential for judgements in general. Kant's remark in the first Critique about 'a blind but indispensable function of the soul' is sometimes enlisted as anticipating the idea of the productive and completely spontaneous 'transcendental imagination' of the third Critique, where aesthetic imagination is the paradigm of what is 'normally hidden in the depth of the human soul'.

This approach goes astray in two distinct but connected ways. It wrongly assumes that Kant's remarks about imagination in the first Critique amount to no more than empirical observations about concept formation. And, secondly, it seems to assume that no mere empirical concept, applicable to experience, can figure in a central role in transcendental arguments. Now it is true that Kant speaks about empirical and transcendental imagination and that he contrasts its empirical and its transcendental use. Certainly he is careless here and positively invites misunderstanding. But rather than taking them too literally, we should read these phrases in the light of Kant's unequivocal conception of a transcendental inquiry into those conditions without which, as he puts it, experience would not be possible. There cannot be two kinds of imagination, empirical and transcendental, nor even two uses or employments of imagination. It is possible, however, to consider the concept of imagination transcendentally, that is to say, we can ask for the conditions that make its empirical employment possible, and we can explore its role, if it has one, in the statement of those conditions that make judgements of experience in general possible. But in either case we must avoid the fundamental error of supposing that there are two kinds of imagination, empirical and transcendental. And it surely must be wrong to think that transcendental arguments make use of special, that is transcendental concepts, while no empirical concepts can occur in them. It is just this, however, that the dualist approach implicitly or explicitly argues when it contrasts the first Critique with the third on the grounds that a progression can be found from empirical to transcendental imagination, or from empirical to transcendental employment of imagination. Such a view fails to understand the notion of a transcendental inquiry in Kant's sense.

(II)

The views I have rejected rely on textual evidence of an ostensibly impressive nature. It is, nevertheless, debatable or controversial evidence. The support for the claim that is characteristic of all three views, namely that imagination bridges various gaps of a metaphysical or psychological kind, is drawn mainly from the Metaphysical Deduction, from those parts of the first edition version of the Transcendental Deduction that constitute what is usually called the Subjective Deduction, and from the Schematism chapter. In order to show why, as I believe, the evidence is of limited or dubious power, I must now say something, however briefly, about the central argument of the first Critique.

The faculty view runs into difficulties about the place of imagination in the Critique. Imagination is, clearly, somehow necessary to Kant's account of the presuppositions of experience. What is required is some attempt to show how the explanation of this role can be reconciled with Kant's explicit statement that sense, understanding and reason between them exhaust the distinctions we have to make in order to exhibit the conditions under which alone knowledge is possible. To see what such an account might be we have to consider the general structure of Kant's argument. *The Critique of Pure Reason* can be thought of as concerned with articulating the consequences of accepting that the percept/concept distinction enters necessarily into any empirical judgement. Thus amongst the conditions under which something is to count as knowledge there will be some that require that evidence should support our knowledge claims, that is conditions for verification in the broadest sense of that term. Kant divided these conditions rather sharply into the demand that something must be given to sense and the demand that there must be something amenable to the understanding. In so far as this expresses a distinction between the perceptual and the conceptual in our analysis of experience, the distinction is one we can easily recognise, though how it is to be drawn in detail is another matter. In addition to these conditions, which Kant explores in the Aesthetic and Analytic respectively, he also speaks of the human capacity to conceive regulative directives for the ordering of knowledge claims and for possibly new ventures in attaining knowledge. This capacity he calls 'reason', which is dangerously given to free-wheeling but indispensable when properly disciplined.

Sense and understanding between them completely cover the distinctions we need to make, at this level of generality, concerning what is required for judgements of experience. There is no room for a third 'faculty' between sense and understanding. The perceptual/conceptual distinction yields adequate criteria for the verifiability of experienced content, and this is so irrespective of whether or not we also admit, as Kant does, reason and the regulative ideas belonging to it as part of the epistemologist's concern. That Kant's points are conceptual ones, then, is fairly clear, and as such they surely cannot be statements about our mental make-up or internal constitution. Nothing is to be gained from thinking of sensibility, understanding, or reason, even in a metaphorical sense, as chief negotiators in personal transactions with the world.

Now, while what is given to sense and what is thought must be distinguishable aspects of empirical judgements, thought about the given presupposes a further condition, that is, an *identity condition*. Experience requires identity of consciousness for which something is given and by which something previously given and thought can be recalled. These two conditions are distinct but intimately related. Both are conditions of experience, though not one homogeneous set of conditions. The percept / concept condition, as I said, enters necessarily into any empirical judgement about experience, but in the Transcendental Deduction Kant draws from this *via* the identity condition the further consequence that experience is necessarily sometimes experience of particulars that exist independently of our experience of them. The connection between these various claims seems to be, summarily, of this nature. If we re-express the percept / concept condition as one to the effect that we must, in experience, be able to recognise sense-particulars as being of a general kind, we are led to see that the possibility of there being any such recognitional element in experience rests on the possibility of attributing different experiences to a single consciousness, to a subject who is aware of them and can ascribe these experiences to himself. But if this is to be possible we must *a fortiori* allow for a contrast between subjective experiences and what these are experiences of, that is to say, a subjective order of experiences distinct from an objective order of things and events of which we can be said to have experience, that is of things which we encounter and re-encounter in experience. Thus the most general requirement that items of experience should be recognisable as being of certain kinds (the percept / concept distinction) yields, when interpreted in the light of the identity condition, the further requirement that the items so recognised should include objects that can be identified and re-identified as persistent objects in the flux of experience. To the requirement that an item or items of experience be subsumable under concepts, we must add the requirement that such items necessarily fall within the experience of a subject preserving an identity through time. For without this condition being satisfied, momentary and fleeting impressions of sense could not be available for concept application to objective particulars at all; and without the notion of an objective particular distinct from our experience of it, we could make no sense of the ascription of *any* experience, objective or not, to a single consciousness. From this conclusion then flow all those consequences concerning the nature of objects as spatio-temporal particulars that Kant adduces.

If this can in any way serve as a summary of a highly complex and rich argument, then the place we must find in it for imagination is just the place that we must assign to the recognitional component in experience. We are here concerned with that special concept of imagination referred to earlier, indicating the ability of a subject of experience to connect or unite discrete impressions of sense – the ability to recognise objects as being of a kind, and particular objects as recurring features of experience. The role of imagination in this technical sense is no mere power of the mind to associate or supplement actual sense perceptions, in Humean fashion, with imagined perceptions resembling them or standing in some orderly external relation to them. The point is rather that the perceptual judgement already implicitly presupposes recognition of identity, that is awareness of identity of an object of *these* experiences with the object of *those* (other) experiences. For the possibility of such recognition is tied to the most general condition of the possibility of thought about reality, namely the unity of the subject of experiences. If experiences are to be accounted mine I must, at least in principle, be able to recognise some of them as experiences of objects distinct from my experience of them, for it is this alone that makes it possible to distinguish between experiences and what has them, that is the subject.

When Kant speaks, then, of experiences as somehow being 'grounded in imagination', we have to resist one or other of two tendencies: we must not think of an image-making power of the mind, working through psychological laws of association with sense impressions to produce the (possibly erroneous) idea of an external object; and we must not succumb to the idea of a power of 'transcendental synthesis' curiously aping, without actually being, an empirical synthesis. No doubt what Kant says can be misleading, but it is not as misleading as this. Kant's

problems are problems about the conditions of concept application to what can be experienced through sense, and they raise
questions about what constitutes *my* experience of a world that
others could experience also.

With this sketch behind us let us return to what I called the
dubious validity of the evidence usually adduced in attempts to
strengthen the account of the alleged gap-bridging role of
imagination, evidence that may now appear in a somewhat
different light. If we agree that with the concept of imagination
Kant has not introduced into the ground plan of the Critique a
new faculty in harness with the others and on the same level
with them, then we shall have to take a closer look at what the
Schematism chapter says about schemata being 'products of the
imagination'. The logical point we here need to acknowledge
follows from what I have just said about 'imagination' in the
technical sense pointing to an identity condition presupposed in
the making of objective knowledge claims. Acknowledging this
point, we might also recognise that schemata, or products of the
imagination, are not extra entities existing obscurely between
percepts and concepts; they are reminders of the requirements
of concept application not just to fleeting experiences, but to
experienced objects in a temporal world. We do not then have to
wonder what schemata *are*, in the way we should if we thought
of them as articles of mental furniture.

The Metaphysical Deduction is one of the main stumbling
blocks to anyone's understanding of Kant. I can do nothing
about this here except to agree with those philosophers who
consider its inclusion in the Critique both unfortunate and ultimately unnecessary. Moreover, I believe that all Kant's points
of substance can be made without reference to it. To argue this
in detail would be a lengthy business. But the exclusion of the
Metaphysical Deduction does not have to rest on any claims
connected with the doctrine of imagination: arguments against
it can be made on more central philosophical grounds. So for
our purposes no questions are being begged by ignoring it. It
does mean, though, that we may allow ourselves to pass over
Kant's most frequently quoted and yet most unilluminating
statement about imagination, namely that it is 'a blind but indispensable function of the soul, without which we should have
no knowledge whatsoever, but of which we are scarcely ever

conscious' (A 78).

This leaves the evidence of the Subjective Deduction, where Kant illustrates the requirements of transcendental unity of apperception by an excursion into an examination of what the subject or agent of experience must in some sense be supposed to do in, or to have done before, an act of cognition. The 'threefold synthesis', that is synthesis of apprehension of intuition, synthesis of reproduction in imagination, and synthesis of recognition in a concept, stresses the active participation of the experiencing subject in the construction of experience; and imagination, in its reproductive capacity, definitely appears in it as a connecting device. Not only that, but Kant here explicitly speaks of a 'faculty': '. . . the reproductive synthesis of the imagination is to be counted among the transcendental acts of the mind. We shall therefore entitle this faculty the transcendental faculty of imagination' (A 102).

It would be difficult for me to ignore such an explicit statement supporting both the psychological and the dualist interpretations of Kant that I have been trying to discredit. But fortunately Kant has done the ignoring for me. When he revised the Critique for the second edition, he left out the entire Subjective Deduction and rewrote the Transcendental Deduction without reference to acts of synthesising done by subjects confronting inchoate data of experience. Clearly Kant was aware of how much he had been misunderstood; it is less clear whether he realised that what he had said in the first edition was not merely misleading but incompatible with the actual message of the Transcendental Deduction. A deduction that began with what looked like a description of mental activities of a cognising subject could not but give the impression that its author was engaged in descriptive psychology, a task at odds with his central inquiry into the logical presuppositions of empirical thought. The Subjective Deduction puts on imagination, understood as a mental capacity for combination and recall, an important share of the burden not only of constructing experience, but of constructing the world, a world that we experience as unified because imagination somehow brings together what would otherwise be a chaotic medley of impressions. On the views contained in these passages from the Subjective Deduction alone, no distinction could be made between what is experienced as real and what is merely imagined. Kant made it look as if the categories were subsequently deduced to yield the conceptual framework for a construct held together by imagination. His second thoughts were better. It seems strange to me that some commentators – Heidegger for example[2] – should take the view that Kant lost his nerve in the second edition and eradicated from it everything that made the Critical doctrine worthwhile.

We can say, therefore, that the approaches to Kant that try to see imagination in the first Critique as a special power with gap-bridging and world-constructing capacities depend heavily on textual evidence that can either be discounted on general philosophical grounds, or be read as making logical points and not points about the actual workings of a complicated mental machinery. If the technical sense of 'imagination' is acceptable at all – and I believe that this is the only way in which Kant's insistence on the necessity of imagination in his transcendental arguments can be reconciled with the overall purpose of the first Critique – then 'imagination' does not refer to a subjective agency for welding together a precarious artifice of experience but to that part of the set of conditions for knowledge claims that the Transcendental Deduction, perhaps not completely successfully, brings to the fore as 'transcendental unity of apperception'.

(III)

Let me now attempt to bring out the point I have been trying to make in a slightly different way. I have been urging, on behalf of Kant, a special role for the concept of imagination that stands in contrast to that of a mere producer of images working in association with sense impressions to construct an idea of the object. That imagination has this latter role in the Subjective Deduction is undeniable, and it is equally undeniable, I think, that in the first edition of the Critique Kant was insufficiently clear about the implications of having a notion of imagination in the sense of a capacity of the mind for forming mental images of that which does not exist or is not now present, whether this be free creative thought or passive delusion or misperception. But imagination as so conceived, far from being instrumental in the formation of a coherent conception of the world of experience, presupposes that we already have such a conception. And the possibility of exercising imagination in this sense of image-making is first established by the argument of the Transcendental Deduction and not already given. This is the point that Kant made in the second edition of the Critique, perhaps in implicit criticism of his first version, the Subjective Deduction.

What Kant realised, then, in the second edition, if not yet clearly in the first, was that if a role for imagination in the analysis of the presuppositions of experience is to be found in the recognition of objects, and of an object as being of a certain kind, as the identity condition requires, thought or experience of such particulars cannot be *constituted by* experiences filled out or supplemented by images formed in the imagination. If this were true, the contrast between 'imagined' and 'known as real or objective' would vanish. Kant actually makes this point in an extended footnote to the Introduction to the second edition, which underlines where the main differences between the two editions of the Critique are to be found (B xl/xli). Kant there contrasts imagination, in one of its ordinary connotations as involving the unreal or delusory, with certain points of the central thesis of the Transcendental Deduction. Dealing with the presuppositions of objectively valid knowledge claims based on experiences, he stresses that consciousness of self requires that we should sometimes be conscious in experience of external, independently existing objects, of an 'outside something'. He says:

> ... the reality of outer sense, in its distinction from imagination, rests simply on that which is there found to take place, namely its being inseparably bound up with inner experience, and the conditions of its possibility.

And later on in the same footnote he continues:

> The reality of outer sense is thus necessarily bound up with inner sense, if experience in general is to be possible at all; that is, I am just as certainly conscious that there are things outside me, which are in relation to my sense, as I am conscious that I myself exist as determined in time. In order to determine to which given intuition objects outside me actually correspond, and which therefore belong to outer *sense* (to which and not to the faculty of imagination, they are to be ascribed), we must in each single case appeal to the rules according to which experience in general, even

inner experience, is distinguished from imagination – the proposition that there is such a thing as outer experience being always presupposed.

In other words, the distinction between what is really experienced and what merely imagined is a distinction we must be able to make if we are to have a coherent conception of experience at all, and the proof of this rests on just those claims of the Transcendental Deduction which, in the Subjective Deduction, presuppose that this distinction has already been made. In these passages, therefore, we have a good indication of the direction in which we should develop a Kantian critique of the empiricist doctrine of imagination as it is exemplified in the philosophy of Hume. Kant did not work out the details; but they are implicit in the overall argument of the second edition of the Critique.

Hume's statement of the empiricist doctrine lays bare a number of ambiguities and puzzles. Hume attempted, indeed felt compelled to attempt, to attribute to imagination whatever unities we are somehow constrained to assume. And since we cannot, according to his doctrine, justify their assumption rationally, all such unities are in the last resort fictitious. Whatever goes beyond the narrow limits of immediate experience and purely logical inference must, according to Hume, be assigned to the imagination. The result is an inability to account for the distinction between experiences of objects and products of the imagination, and, we might add, between imagination and memory images.

Being debarred – by his own doctrine of what alone we can be certain of – from making the natural distinction in terms of experience of the real world and merely subjective experience, Hume had to find a distinguishing criterion in terms of qualitative differences within subjective experience. His proposals in terms of vivacity or liveliness of impressions, and relative coherence and incoherence of ideas, not surprisingly failed to provide such a criterion. As Kant saw clearly, the distinction between experience of something independent of the experiencer and just experience cannot be made in terms of qualitative differences, if any, of these experiences themselves. For what is important here are not the qualities of impressions or ideas, but the possible reference of at least some of these impressions or ideas to a world of public objects. And a set of rules that would allow us to make such distinctions cannot itself be an item of experience or derived from a qualitative differentiation of subjective experience. If we had to see the world in Humean, radically phenomenalist, terms, Kant could say, we should no longer have a coherent conception of experience at all, because we should not be able to distinguish between ourselves and the experiences we have. It would then follow that we could not distinguish between real and imagined things, and, for the same reason, talking about objective and non-objective experience would not make sense. Hume, who certainly struggled with these difficulties, could not but make imagination play a role that is basically incoherent. On the one hand, it is the only means we have on his view of constructing unities out of atomic and unrelated 'givens', unities we need, however, in order to say the most elementary things we do say about our experiences beyond the solipsistic ones of the present moment. On the other hand, imagined unities remain rationally suspect. So imagination supplies what sensation and ideas cannot guarantee; but the products of imagination, in so far as they simulate an 'as-if' permanence and continuity of our world, cannot be distinguished from merely fanciful inventions of the free-wheeling imagination. It is little wonder, then, that Hume in one breath asserts the indispensability of the imagination *and* its unreliability and dangers. The unreliability claim, however, is very odd; for Hume cannot, given his own assumptions, specify what it would be to have reliable perceptions and cognitions of enduring things in this world, including persons, without imagination playing a vital role.

Now Kant may not have entirely escaped Hume's difficulties in the earlier stages of his Critical philosophy. There are many passages in the first edition of the *Critique of Pure Reason* that raise just those problems which disturb us in Hume. But the second edition makes it clearer why these problems arose and where we must look for a solution to them. Kant's Refutation of Idealism, for instance, aims at showing, among other things, that subjective idealism must be incoherent. And if that argument is correct, Humean phenomenalism is equally ruled out, because it could avoid solipsism only at the cost of regarding all objectivity as fictitious, as product of the imagination in the sense of 'seeing what is not really there'. We should then be left without the means of drawing a contrast between what we think of as imagined and what we think of as perceived; but this is precisely the distinction that is required for coherent thought about experience. As Kant says in the Refutation: 'The required proof must, therefore, show that we have *experience*, and not merely imagination of outer things . . .' (B 275).

Kant's Transcendental Deduction in the second edition is a sustained attempt to provide just such a proof. The details cannot concern us here. For they deal not with imagination, but with that with which imagination can and must be contrasted, namely experience of an objective world in space and time.

To conclude then this inquiry into Kant's views on imagination we might say this. The distinction between what is perceived and what is imagined cannot be made if what we think or believe we perceive is in large part already supplied by imagination. Yet this distinction is one we not only do make but have to be able to make. We can make it, I believe, in terms of the main argument of the *Critique of Pure Reason*. That such a distinction must be possible is, however, not merely a requirement within Kant's philosophy. It is a claim that must be argued in any philosophical context in which problems of imagination arise. Imagination must, in an important sense, be parasitic upon experience of a real, non-imagined world. Kant's arguments in the first Critique go a long way towards showing that the possibility of imagining things depends on experience being at least sometimes experience of a real world of objects in space and time. The possibility that we sometimes experience a world of external objects is a condition of our being able sometimes to imagine both things that do not exist and things other than they are.

Judgements about these latter situations in which imagination plays a role that removes such judgements from the range of empirical knowledge claims form the main subject matter of the third Critique. My reason for having here dealt mainly with the *Critique of Pure Reason* is that I believe that the issues I have discussed that are related to this Critique have to be clarified before the third Critique's concern with imagination can begin to make sense.

Epistemological Claims
and Judgements of Taste

Kant's analysis of the judgement of taste in the third Critique raises many problems, both in what it says (or fails to say) about the judgement of taste itself, and in the place it assigns to it among other species of judgement. It may, then, appear somewhat perverse to suggest that what Kant holds about judgements of taste might be illuminated by a series of comparisons with an even more problematic distinction in his philosophy, that is, the distinction between judgements of experience and judgements of perception. Nevertheless, the comparisons are, I believe, worth exploring, and they constitute the theme of this discussion.

(I)

Judgements of Taste and the A Priori. Judgements of taste would differ in an obvious way from other judgements which we might (as yet without Kantian connotations) call judgements of experience if they were in fact not *a posteriori* or empirical judgements at all. There are indeed passages in the *Critique of Judgement* where, telescoping a number of points into one statement, Kant seems to be saying just that: judgements of taste are *a priori* judgements. Many readers simply take it for granted that this is a central feature of Kant's aesthetics. To mention just one commentator, John Kemp in his outline of Kant's aesthetics attributes to Kant the unequivocal view that 'aesthetic judgements are necessary and *a priori*', and 'it is clear that they must be synthetic'.[1] Bizarre as such a view is, there must be some grounds in Kant for this attribution, and we do not have to look far for the evidence. Take, for example, this extract from § 37 (289):

A judgement to the effect that it is with pleasure that I perceive and estimate some object is an empirical judgement. But if I assert that I think the object beautiful, i.e. that I may attribute that delight to every one as necessary, it is then an *a priori* judgement.

Faced with such a passage as this, we might well feel that Kant's contributions to philosophy elsewhere are not matched by his treatment of aesthetic appraisals. Either what he claims is simply false, or it introduces a conception of the *a priori* for which even his prolific uses of that term in earlier works have scarcely prepared us. But Kant nowhere suggests that the sense of the term '*a priori*' is in any way peculiar to the third Critique. He must, then, be wrong if we take what he says at face value. For even if, negatively speaking, we have qualms about calling such verdicts as 'this rose is beautiful' straightforwardly empirical in the sense in which 'this rose has a penetrating scent' certainly is, we are not ready to concede full-blown *a priori* status to them either.

On the other hand, even a moderately sympathetic consideration of Kant's arguments in the Critique of Aesthetic Judgement as a whole leaves one with the impression that what we have here is not a statement of a position that is clearly false, but rather an inaccurate version of a view that, if not clearly true, is not altogether wrong either. In the § 37 passage Kant must have been tempted by the fact (or what, in the light of his investigations in the Analytic of the Beautiful, he saw as a fact) that judgements of taste lay claim to universal assent, that is 'that I may attribute that delight to every one as necessary', to assign *a priori* status to the very judgements of which this fact is true. For, of course, on standard Kantian doctrine, universality and necessity are the 'marks' of the *a priori*. But the inference that all judgements that in some way involve universality and necessity claims must themselves be *a priori* is fallacious: the relationship between judgements and their presuppositions is more complex than this simple conflation suggests. Moreover, in other places Kant is not tempted to merge the two claims. Thus, in the Transcendental Deduction of the first Critique, Kant does not say of his example 'bodies are heavy' that it is a necessary *a priori* truth just because its being true (or false) requires the truth of certain *a priori* principles that govern the making of objective knowledge claims; on the contrary, he says that that judgement 'is itself empirical, and therefore contingent' (*Critique of Pure Reason*, § 19, B 142).

It is sufficient, then, for Kant's purposes to concede that a claim to universality and necessity indicates that *a priori* principles are *somehow* involved, perhaps in the sense that judgements that 'lay claim' to universality and necessity are grounded on non-empirically derived principles that supply the necessary pre-suppositions for our being able to make such judgements at all. The elucidation of such principles is, after all, what the Critical philosophy in general is about.

Kant's own distinction between what we say *de facto* and what *de jure* when applied to judgements on the agreeable and judgements of taste is of some help here. The certificate of authenticity for judgements on the agreeable, to adapt a phrase from the first Critique, is simply that of truth to personal experience or factual verification: to the extent that we can make generalisations at all about what groups of people at a given time or individuals at different times prefer, these will at best be empirical statements derived from observations of personal preferences. It may even be, Kant allows, that judgements of taste can form the basis of generalisations about what people in a group or society of individuals over a period of time in fact judge to be beautiful. The difference between these two kinds of aesthetic judgement (of which judgements of taste are of central importance) lies elsewhere. For it is a *necessary* feature of judgements of taste, as it is not of judgements on the merely pleasing, that they lay claim to the agreement of others and as such require a certificate of authenticity quite different from that of judgements on the agreeable. Our entitlement to make them has to be differently established. Moreover, this certificate must be awarded on grounds other than those that Kant finds operative in the non-subjective knowledge claims about the world as revealed in experience with which the first Critique deals. The problem of the Critique of Aesthetic Judgement is to provide a justification of the claim to universal validity that yet preserve this essential distinction between judgements of taste and objective knowledge claims. The justification must be in non-empirical terms, appealing to something like laws or prescriptions. Judgements claiming to hold good for everyone need not themselves be *a priori* judgements – few in fact are; but they must be based on principles that can show what they claim to be justifiable. The implicit 'ought' in judgements of taste, which, whilst not a moral 'ought', lends them the verdict character that judgements on the agreeable conspicuously lack, is definitely an indication that such commitments must be transcendentally justified. This is also the reason why Kant thinks that judgements of taste require a deduction, as do the *de jure* claims of the *Critique of Pure Reason*.

Lewis White Beck has suggested in a short paper[2] that Kant's unsatisfactory formulations of the role of the *a priori* in judgements of taste, as exemplified in § 37, can be clarified in terms of an analogy with a distinction Kant makes in the *Prolegomena* (§§ 18–20) between judgements of perception and judgements of experience. The analogy spans that distinction and the distinction in the Critique of Aesthetic Judgement between judgements on the agreeable and judgements on the beautiful that lies at the centre of Kant's alternative to the traditional aesthetic of likes and dislikes. The analogy works, Beck thinks, because both distinctions seem to be grounded in a contrast between the *a posteriori* and the *a priori*. To see how the analogy proceeds we have to remember the controversial points Kant makes in the *Prolegomena* about judgements of perception and judgements of experience. The former are subjectively valid, the latter objectively so, and the former do not, as do the latter, involve the application of categories or *a priori* concepts to experience. Beck's interest lies just here, in the implication, or lack of it, of categorial application, for it is here, he thinks, that the *a posteriori*/*a priori* contrast gets a grip.

We can spell out his view in this way. If it is true that judgements of perception do not involve the application of categories (and this is a controversial point, but we may leave it on one side for the time being) then we cannot think of them as making knowledge claims. Judgements of experience, on the other hand, as involving categorial application, certainly do make knowledge claims. And the way they do, Beck argues, can throw light on the way in which judgements of taste claim universal agreement *of necessity*, or, as Kant puts it, unsatisfactorily, are somehow *a priori*. For to say that judgements of experience are knowledge claims implies that something is claimed to be true, and, if true, such judgements must be agreed upon necessarily by everybody. The necessity here lies in the imputation of agreement, not in the judgement itself. Once this is seen, an analogous point can be made about the way necessity is involved in judgements of taste. Judgements of taste, though not themselves *a priori* judgements, have *a priori* commitments.

Had Kant seen the analogy, Beck supposes, he would have been able greatly to clarify, and provide a more satisfactory account of, the relation of judgements of taste to the *a priori*. Kant, on this diagnosis, correctly notes that there is an *a priori* connection between the claim to universality and necessity and judgements of taste, and also that there is a significant conceptual difference between judgements on the agreeable and judgements on the beautiful (judgements of taste). But in taking the first point to be an explanation or reason for the second, he proceeds to apply the *a posteriori / a priori* distinction directly to the two kinds of judgements themselves: judgements on the agreeable are empirical and *a posteriori*, judgements on the beautiful are *a priori*. Hence the stumbling block of § 37.

We can now set this passage to rights, Beck proposes, by the simple expedient of replacing the 'i.e.' by a 'thus', so making the attribution of delight to everyone as necessary an inference from, rather than a gloss upon, what 'this is beautiful' means – as contrasted with 'this pleases me', in accordance with the arguments of the Analytic of the Beautiful. The apparent conclusion – 'it is then an *a priori* judgement' – can now be read as a statement not about a particular judgement of taste such as 'this is beautiful', but about what Beck calls 'a theoretical judgement in the meta-language of aesthetics'. Although Beck does not say what the statement in the meta-language would be, it is clear enough that what is *a priori* must be the statement of the principle or principles presupposed by a judgement of taste, or, in Kantian terms, a statement in transcendental logic of what makes such a judgement possible. What we now have, then, in place of the baldly false claim that aesthetic judgements are *a priori* is the interesting suggestion that there are certain things we can say *a priori* in aesthetic theory that back up a conceptual feature of judgements of taste themselves, namely that they lay claim to universal agreement or validity. What is *a priori* are neither statements of the form 'x is beautiful' nor statements about universal validity alone, but principles justifying the connection between the two.

So far Beck's analogy can be used to bring out in a helpful way what must surely be on any considered view Kant's attitude to the role of the *a priori* in judgements in general. But how much further can the analogy be taken ? Judgements of taste and judgements of experience are indeed comparable in that it is a feature of both kinds of judgement that, when correct, they can legitimately claim that others should and must agree. So in each case something must hold that justifies such a claim. In the case of particular empirical judgements which make knowledge claims, that is, in the case of what Kant in the *Prolegomena* calls 'judgements of experience', this is provided by the categorial framework. Whatever facts guarantee the truth of such judgements (and this is an empirical matter), that everyone must agree to them as facts is secured by the application of the categories, for these alone allow judgements to be objective. If, then, some empirical judgement p is true (or false), then it must be true (or false) for everyone. This, of course, does not make p a necessary or universal proposition, or necessarily true or false. As an empirical proposition p is contingent (and particular, let us assume), but assent to its truth or falsity can be claimed of necessity from all. Now an individual judgement of taste also may be correct or incorrect, though not in the same way as an empirical judgement; but whatever guarantees its correctness (a large question Beck does not discuss), *if* it is correct we can claim that it must be so for everyone. And this must be because of principles that hold *a priori*, analogously to the categories and categorial principles that hold for empirical knowledge claims. These principles must figure in Kant's analysis of the ground of judgements of taste in the principle of pleasure or displeasure. In both cases – particular empirical judgements of experience and individual aesthetic judgements of taste – the 'marks of the *a priori*' (universality and necessity) must be taken as marks of the *a priori* in the principles or presuppositions that justify and make intelligible the claim to universal agreement.

So far the analogy has held up fairly well, but what it fails to take account of is the crucial difference between judgements of experience and judgements of taste : the latter, unlike the former, are *subjective*. It is doubtless correct, in general, to say that if some empirical judgement is true, then it can command universal assent of necessity (and similarly, dissent if it is false). But what are we to say about what corresponds or should correspond in the sphere of aesthetics to false empirical judgements ? That is, granted a specific judgement of taste is 'in order', what should we say about those that are not ? Can there indeed be any such ? Here the analogy with empirical knowledge claims seems to be pushed beyond the limit, for there are specific and important differences between aesthetic and cognitive judgements that have been ignored in the account so far given. Consider, for example, § 19 of the Analytic of the Beautiful. It begins with the confident claim that 'the judgement of taste exacts agreement from every one'. And this is what one would expect, of course. For whether the judgement is correct or incorrect, simply in its character as a judgement of taste it lays claim to agreement, though, we must add, without any likelihood of enforcing it. But there is, Kant insists, a big difference between cognitive empirical judgements on the one hand and aesthetic judgements on the other: among the former, we can, and indeed must, distinguish between those that command assent because they are not only claimed to be true, but are true, and those that make this claim but are not borne out by the facts. On the other hand, judgements of taste, *qua* judgements of taste, always claim agreement but can never enforce it in the way in that true empirical judgements must always in principle be able to do. The correctness or incorrectness of a judgement on the beautiful, if it can be shown at all, cannot be shown in the way in which the truth or falsity of an empirical judgement can be demonstrated. In § 19 Kant actually ends on a note strongly emphasising this contrast rather than the similarity with judgements of experience:

> Further, we would be able to count on this agreement, provided we were always assured of the correct subsumption of the case under that ground as the rule of approval. (237)

The difficulty here lies not in knowing when a subsumption has been correctly made, but what the phrase 'correct subsumption' can mean in the context of aesthetic estimates or appraisals, approval or disapproval. This is one feature which distinguishes the aesthetic from the cognitive sphere not only in Kant's aesthetics but in almost every account that admits talk about something specifically aesthetic at all. It is a difference which Kant chooses to mark by assigning to aesthetic judgements subjective validity only. Knowledge claims embodied in judgements of experience in the *Prolegomena* sense, on the other hand, have objective validity. Indeed, when we say that an empirical judgement, when true, commands universal assent of necessity, we say no more and no less than that it is objectively valid. Criteria for truth are available, or, as Kant would say, rules for the correct subsumption of the experienced items under concepts can be provided. When we come to aesthetic judgements such rules and criteria are absent, or where they exist they are empirically obtained from the aesthetic judgements already circulating. There is no established mode of verification or falsification as there is for empirical judgements generally. This is what Kant means by saying they have only subjective validity. That is not to say, however, that they are therefore defective – they are just different in kind.

Once Kant's distinction between subjective and objective validity as it applies to judgements of taste is brought in, the limitations of Beck's analogy immediately become apparent. Objective validity and the criteria for this only form the basis of the analogy he proposes. Of course it is not the contrast between subjective and objective but rather that between the *a posteriori* and the *a priori* which holds the centre of the stage in Beck's account, for he wishes to show how it is not judgements of taste that are themselves *a priori*, but certain statements in the meta-language of aesthetic theory. And here certainly he can point to the parallel with empirical judgements that Kant in the *Prolegomena* calls judgements of experience: they too are not themselves *a priori* although they involve principles of Kantian metaphysics that are. So the other side of the *Prolegomena* distinction, that featuring judgements of perception, does not really figure prominently. These judgements have no *a priori* presuppositions, not even indirect ones, and in this respect they are comparable to judgements upon the agreeable and the merely pleasing. No claim that everyone should agree with them, let alone that one should do so of necessity, can arise. So whilst judgements of perception and judgements of experience are seen by Beck to stand to each other in something like the way judgements on the agreeable stand to judgements of taste, the relationship between the first two items in the two contrasts is left unprobed.

Someone might be tempted to conclude from Beck's analogy that since Kant's judgements of perception are subjectively valid only, whilst judgements of experience are objectively valid, an analogous treatment of judgements in aesthetic theory will yield a parallel distinction between merely subjectively valid judgements on the agreeable and objectively valid judgements of taste. This, however, would be a serious mistake. Kant states repeatedly and unambiguously that judgements on the agreeable and judgements of taste alike are subjectively valid and that the universality and necessity claimed for judgements of taste also are merely subjective. *Both* types of aesthetic judgement stand in sharp contrast to the cognitive judgements of experience; both are denied the status of knowledge claims.

If the *Prolegomena* distinction, then, is to provide any further illumination of Kant's judgements of taste, more light must be shed in the dark corners of Kant's account of judgements of perception, for it is here, if anywhere, and not in his account of judgements of experience, that we find the notion of subjective validity at least prepared for. At the same time we must not lose sight of the important point that Beck's analogy emphasises: that judgements of taste share with cognitive judgements of experience the commitment to *a priori* grounds that lifts them out of the sphere of merely private likes and dislikes.

(II)

Judgements of Taste and Subjective Validity. Kant's distinction between 'subjective' and 'objective' is a striking example of extreme parsimony in the use of key terms by a philosopher who is so often accused of a tendency to multiply technical terms beyond necessity. Part of the difficulty for his readers is that this distinction is put to work in different contexts that only indirectly illuminate one another. The illumination is there nevertheless; and we cannot hope to penetrate Kant's use of the contrast in the *Critique of Judgement* without examining its employment in other areas of the Critical philosophy. Problems about the notion of a subjectively valid judgement arise not only in connection with aesthetic judgements but also with perceptual judgements or judgements based on them. Our attitude towards aesthetic judgements will not be unaffected by our attitude towards those judgements that in the philosophical tradition are held typically to report what one is directly aware of or immediately acquainted with in perception, and the knowledge claims to which they might be thought to give rise or which they might be considered to make possible.

As a first attempt at a characterisation of subjectively valid judgements we might say that a judgement can be subjectively valid in at least two senses: (a) it is somehow about or of a subject who judges rather than about an object on which judgement is passed, and (b) it need hold only for the individual who makes the judgement and is thus not binding on others. In general, and with Kant's distinctions within the class of aesthetic judgements left on one side, it is indeed commonly recognised that there is something peculiar about aesthetic judgements, appraisals, assessments, or estimates (which I take to be more or less synonymous with Kant's *Urteil* on matters aesthetic); and (a) and (b) seem to give some sort of rationale to this peculiarity. For there is a marked absence of general principles to which to appeal when one wants to show that a given aesthetic appraisal, assessment, estimate or judgement is the right one: there is no proof of aesthetic rightness or correctness that takes the form of demonstrating what follows from a general rule in conjunction with a description of the relevant features of the object judged – as is the case when the judgement is a cognitive or empirical one (compare (b)). Rather, appeal is made essentially to *how* something is experienced, and this may be expressed by saying that an aesthetic appraisal has a strongly subjective element (compare (a)). The absence of agreed general principles and the stress on felt experience is not, however, to be taken to mean that aesthetic judgements of taste must be purely arbitrary. Subjective they might be, but not, at least as we understand aesthetic judgements today, necessarily idiosyncratic. It is in something like this modern sense that Kant speaks of such judgements as 'subjectively valid'.

An aesthetic attribution, then (for example 'this vase is lovely', 'this movement is graceful', 'this picture is beautiful'), implies, or at any rate is based upon, an awareness of how something appears to a person in the act of experiencing it. The element of 'it is so for me' cannot be eliminated. Here grammatical appearances are deceptive. Grammatically, aesthetic attributions take the form of ascribing qualities to, or predicating properties of, objects. But aesthetic ascription logically differs from non-aesthetic ascription or predication in important ways. Whilst non-aesthetic property ascription centres on qualities or properties that are normally perceived as belonging to objects, aesthetic predication centres on what are sometimes called 'emergent' qualities or properties – although such properties need not be understood as consequent only upon aesthetic modes of awareness. They are qualities or properties that we ascribe to objects when a number of structural features in conjunction are experienced as configurations, and this requires acts of concentrated attention or contemplation. Thus terms such as 'round', 'heavy', 'red', 'dark' and 'loud', which are typically used in non-aesthetic ascriptions, are frequently contrasted with aesthetic terms such as 'beautiful', 'lovely', 'graceful', 'hideous', 'garish' and 'ugly'. Using the objective-subjective contrast here, we might say that non-aesthetic qualities can be ascribed in objectively valid judgements because such qualities really belong to objects and this is what these judgements claim irrespective of the observer's role in the making of them; but aesthetic qualities are ascribed in subjectively valid judgements because what the aesthetic judgement states does not hold irrespective of a reference to the observer's peculiar involvement in the judgement. Hence to judge something as having aesthetic properties or qualities that are configurationally 'emergent' is to admit that such judgements are subjectively valid in sense (a), for in their dependence on the experiential capacities and the sensibility of the subject they are, in the relevant sense, 'about' the subject.

Similarly, that they are subjectively valid in sense (b), when this is spelled out in detail, follows directly from the contrast between non-aesthetic and aesthetic property ascription. A non-aesthetic property ascription in an empirical or cognitive judgement must be open to observational monitoring or checking by others, for the ascription is made independently of how the object strikes the observer, even if his experiential involvement is what gives rise to the judgement in the first place. But if an aesthetic property ascription or an attribution of 'emergent' qualities depends on how something appears to a subject in a particular experience, then there is no logical guarantee that others will or must agree on the ascription made if it is to be 'true to the facts'. For there are no facts against which a judgement can be straightforwardly confirmed or tested by independent observers. Others may not experience the object in the same way, or may fail to see any, or the same, aesthetic properties 'emerging' from the conjunction of observable features. If, then, we are to speak at all of the 'verification' of aesthetic ascriptions, it must be in a different sense from that relevant to non-aesthetic judgements. Non-aesthetic judgements can be provided with truth conditions of the strict kind for the ascription of qualities or properties: verification is a matter of checking whether the conditions hold, and this usually proceeds in the case of empirical judgements by an appeal to intersubjective circumstances. But if aesthetic judgements do not ascribe straightforwardly observable properties to objects, then they cannot be given truth conditions for correct ascription. No enumeration of non-aesthetic qualities verified in the normal way entails that the object will be experienced as, for example, beautiful or ugly. 'Subjectively valid' not only connotes negatively 'not objectively valid'; it also, positively, underlines the importance of the personal experience. Second-hand reports are just second-hand.

We might seek to give at least *prima facie* intelligibility to the Kantian idea of a subjectively valid judgement in aesthetic contexts in this way. 'Subjective' as opposed to 'objective' validity serves to locate what, in a rough sketch of the landscape of aesthetic concepts, seem to be the notable peculiarities of aesthetic judgements. But closer scrutiny uncovers problems that need to be resolved before we can say with any confidence that what Kant calls judgements of taste, or what more recently have come to be included in what we call 'aesthetic judgements', may fruitfully be described as subjectively valid.

To mention first a quintessentially Kantian problem: it is not even clear that Kant's philosophy has room for subjectively valid *judgements*. The validity of judgements seems so often simply to be the same as their objectivity. The central argument of the *Critique of Pure Reason*, the Transcendental Deduction, maintains that concepts of a certain kind, categories, are necessary to all knowledge claims, and judgements here seem indistinguishable from knowledge claims. Moreover, the question of how these special concepts can be shown to apply *objectively* receives its Kantian answer that shows how they are required for *knowledge*, which itself requires the distinction between the objective and the subjective: knowledge just is what is expressed in objectively valid judgements. So the notion of a subjectively valid *judgement* takes on the appearance of a contradiction in terms in Kant's philosophy. If knowledge, however defined, must in principle be verifiable, it cannot include within its scope 'subjectively valid' claims in sense (*b*). Even if sense (*a*) were admitted to leave room for 'subjective knowledge' as a kind resulting from privileged access to one's own inner experience, it is doubtful whether this is something Kant could have accepted without qualms or considerable reservations. His theory of knowledge was designed, for one thing, to avoid the difficulties that arise for those who seek to systematise know- ledge on the basis of terminal judgements on the incorrigible data of immediate sense perception, the data of 'inner sense'.

Nevertheless, if we attribute to Kant, as Kemp Smith[3] does for example, the view that to make judgements at all is to make a knowledge claim which is publicly verifiable – that is that the validity of all judgements is objective validity – it is very strange that Kant should follow up the *Critique of Pure Reason* with lengthy treatises on moral and aesthetic *judgements*, and argue that a central feature of them is that neither can be knowledge claims. This alone should make us wary of dismissing too lightly a category of subjectively valid judgements. It is possible, of course, that Kant was muddled and inconsistent; but this would have to come, if at all, as the conclusion of detailed discussion. In any case it is not all that clear, despite voices to the contrary, that the first Critique forecloses the issue.

If we leave on one side for the moment the special problems of Kantian exegesis, we might wonder whether, more generally, the idea of a subjectively valid judgement is viable. We should at least allow that some philosophers find difficulty with it. Wittgenstein's famous remark that 'an "inner process" stands in need of outward criteria', that is criteria that others also could use, points to one difficulty in accepting a class of judgements on purely private items of awareness and personal feeling – a difficulty already perhaps indicated in the first Critique, where Kant speaks of 'the reality of outer sense' being inseparably bound up with inner experience 'as the condition of its possibility' (B xl).[4] If that is right, what is meant by subjective validity in sense (*b*)? If, on the other hand, we think of so-called subjectively valid judgements, again along Wittgensteinian lines, in terms of personal avowals of emotion or feeling, there is some doubt about whether 'validity' is a term that applies to them at all: they are not the sort of utterance that is open either to verification or falsification.

(III)

The Prolegomena Distinction. We can gain an entry into these problems, as they concern Kant, by returning once more to the *Prolegomena* passage (§§ 18–20) in which the distinction between judgements of perception and judgements of experience is made. For this passage contains Kant's most explicit and also most controversial statement of the contrast between subjective and objective validity. To cut short one element of controversy: there are *prima facie* reasons for taking this passage seriously – and not only because the *Prolegomena*, written between editions A and B of the first Critique, is Kant's considered summary of the first version of that Critique. The neatness of the distinction between the purely perceptual and the more complex interplay of the perceptual and the conceptual in experience might be thought to throw some light on how the *Critique of Pure Reason* should be read *vis-à-vis* the division between Aesthetic and Analytic, that is, between sense-givenness and categorial structuring. At the same time I am aware that there are also reasons for thinking that the *Prolegomena* was superseded by the second edition of the Critique, in which the distinction does not appear as such.

First, however, a further comment is in order about Kant's use of the term 'judgement'. When Kant speaks of 'judgements', in whatever context, he does not seem to have linguistic acts primarily in mind. This is one reason why he often reads oddly to the modern ear. Where we are apt to think of judgements as linguistic utterances, Kant pays only slight attention to the verbal expression of thoughts – as everyone who has struggled with his wayward examples will readily testify. His position is better captured by our thinking of the linguistic formulations as, so to speak, *transparent*, something to be 'seen through' to the mental acts 'behind' them, to the experiences they 'reflect'. Thus where we are inclined to think of knowledge in terms of knowledge claims expressed in propositions with which judgement is then equated, Kant thinks rather of the mental activity or experience on the basis of which such judgements are made. Hence it seems natural to him, but not to us, to speak of 'knowledge' in the plural (*Erkenntnisse*), meaning the experiences that ground knowledge claims. It is well known that Kant frequently speaks of one kind of judgement being 'contained' or 'included' in another. It is the experiences that are so included, not their linguistic expressions. This 'containment' language is often severely criticised. But it loses some of its objectionable features when Kant's use of 'judgement' and its implications are understood. Some of his strange-sounding remarks in what follows should therefore be read with this tendency of his to identify judgements and experiences firmly in mind. 'Judgements of perception' and 'judgements of experience' can thus designate mental events in the phenomenology of which Kant is more interested than in their expression in linguistic structures. And in discussing his examples we have to think more of the spirit in which they are offered than of their precise linguistic formulation.

In §§ 18–20 of the *Prolegomena* then, Kant distinguishes between two kinds of empirical judgements: judgements of perception (*Wahrnehmungsurteile*) and judgements of experience (*Erfahrungsurteile*). The subjective validity of the former is firmly linked with the absence of that categorial application which is the hallmark of the latter. The two kinds of judgements are said to be related in that judgements of perception are sometimes, though not always, convertible into judgements of experience, and judgements of experience are said to 'arise from' judgements of perception. So Kant says in § 18:

> *Empirical judgements, so far as they have objective validity*, are JUDGEMENTS OF EXPERIENCE; those which are *only subjectively valid* I call mere JUDGEMENTS OF PERCEPTION. The latter do not need a pure concept of the understanding but only the logical connection of perception in a thinking subject. The former on the other hand always need, in addition to the representation of sensible intuition,

special *concepts originally generated in the understanding*, and it is these that make the judgements of experience *objectively valid*.

All our judgements are at first mere judgements of perception, they are valid only for us, i.e. for our subject, and only afterwards do we give them a new reference, namely to an object, and want the judgement to be valid for us at all times and equally for everybody. . . .

Kant, then, introduced subjectively valid judgements in terms of a contrast with objectively valid ones, and it is the latter that receive the more positive and more detailed characterisation. As we saw earlier, to say that a judgement is objectively valid is to say that it has necessary universal validity, and to say that a judgement is necessarily universally valid is just to say that it is objectively valid. For 'if a judgement agrees with an object, all judgements about the same object must agree with one another, and thus the objective validity of the judgement of experience means nothing other than its necessary universal validity.'

So to hold that a judgement is objectively valid is to say that it is necessarily 'valid for us at all times and equally for everybody'. Conversely, if there is reason to believe that a judgement is necessarily universally valid, we *ipso facto* have reason to believe that it is objectively valid, that is

it expresses not merely a reference of the perception to a subject, but a quality of the object; for there would be no reason why the judgement of others should necessarily agree to mine if it were not for the unity of the object to which all refer, with which they agree and hence must agree with one another. (§ 18)

Objective validity and necessary universal validity thus amount to the same thing: they are, in Kant's phrase, 'identical concepts' (§ 19).

To say that a judgement is subjectively valid, by contrast, is to say that it is 'valid only for us, i.e. for our subject'. It is to disclaim all implications that result from an assertion of objective validity. Judgements of perception, subjectively valid judgements, 'need only the logical connection of perception in the thinking subject', and this, again in contrast to objectively valid judgements, means that they have no commitment to categorial application.

Not least of the problems to which this brief characterisation gives rise is the relationship that Kant sees between the two kinds of empirical judgement. He says that judgements of experience 'have their ground in immediate sense perception', but in addition to the sensible intuitions they involve categories of the understanding 'under which the perception is subsumed'. Now if the objectively valid judgements of experience have their ground in, or rest on, immediate sense perception, this must surely mean that they have their ground in the kind of experience that is recorded in the subjectively valid judgements of perception. And indeed Kant explicitly says: 'All our judgements are at first mere judgements of perception, . . . and only afterwards do we give them a new reference, namely to an object . . .'.

This highly compressed statement is also highly ambiguous. We can glean some hint as to how it might be construed by looking at some of Kant's examples to illustrate the corollary of his claim that though 'all judgements of experience are first judgements of perception', it is not the case that all judgements of perception can be converted into, or form the basis for, judgements of experience. As examples of subjectively valid judgements of perception that cannot be converted in this way Kant suggests: (1) 'this room is warm'; 'sugar is sweet'; 'wormwood is nasty'. As an example of a judgement of perception that can be converted he gives: (2) 'when the sun shines on the stone, the stone grows warm'. This, he thinks, can form the basis for the objectively valid judgement of experience: (3) 'the sun warms the stone'. Here the categories involved in giving our perceptions a 'new reference' to objects prominently include that of causality. Kant explains why he thinks members of group (1) cannot be converted in this way: 'because they refer merely to feeling, which everyone recognises as subjective and which can never be attributed to the object, and thus they can never become objective' (§ 19). If this explanation seems suspect, we can get further illumination from a passage in the *Logik* (§ 40)[5] where the point is made in more perspicuous form. Here Kant argues that, while a judgement of perception is purely subjective (subjectively valid), 'an objective judgement out of perceptions [*aus Wahrnehmungen*] is a judgement of experience'. In a note to this passage he explains that a judgement of mere perception is nevertheless a judgement, although in it one only states one's perceptions as perceptions:

> I, who perceive a tower, perceive in it the red colour. But I cannot say: it is red. For that would not only be an empirical judgement, but a judgement of experience [*Erfahrungs-urteil*], that is to say, an empirical judgement whereby I gain a concept of the object. For instance, 'when I touch the stone, I feel warmth' is a judgement of perception, whilst 'the stone is warm' is a judgement of experience. It belongs to the latter that I do not ascribe to the object what is merely in my subject, for a judgement of experience is the perception which yields a concept of the object.

In many ways this is an improvement on the *Prolegomena* remarks, and Kant clearly has the same distinction in mind. If we read the *Logik* passage as a gloss on the *Prolegomena*, Kant's examples (1) and (2) can be amended to give a less baffling picture. Whereas 'this room is warm' and 'sugar is sweet' hardly seem to fit the characterisation of judgements of perception which cannot be converted, 'I feel warm' and 'this tastes sweet to me' seem to correspond fairly closely to Kant's intentions. Again, Kant's example (2) of a judgement of perception that can, but need not, issue in a judgement of experience, gains in intelligibility if we supplement it from the *Logik*: 'when I touch the stone (on which the sun has been shining) I feel the stone as warm' yields a judgement of experience when the category of cause and effect is brought into play – 'the sun warms the stone'.

In the light of these examples one way of construing Kant's claim that 'all our judgements are at first mere judgements of perception . . . and only afterwards do we give them a new reference, namely to an object . . .' might be this. Judgements of perception report the having of perceptions of certain kinds, while judgements of experience attribute properties to, or relations between, items perceived. If I report simply how something strikes me – even if this something is designated by an object term (e.g. 'sugar', 'room', 'wormwood', etc.) – as in '*x* looks red to me' or '*x* feels warm to me', I am not *ipso facto* saying something about how the object is. For how an object is may be otherwise than how it strikes me. We have to add, however, that how the object is eventually judged to be is not, and cannot

be, totally independent of how it strikes someone as being, for
what first discloses the object is, after all, a perception of it. So
when I assert that a certain object has a certain property, or
stands in a certain relationship to something else, it is because
I am having, or have had, certain perceptions, or at least this is
true of someone. In this way all judgements of experience are
ultimately justified by perceptions that a person who arrives at
objectively valid judgements has had or at least could have. This
might be what Kant means when he says that judgements of
experience are judgements 'out of' perceptions (in the *Logik*)
and that 'all judgements of experience are first judgements of
perception' (*Prolegomena*). Seen in this way, a possible judgement of perception would be the evidential basis for the truth of
a given judgement of experience. Such a view seems innocuous
enough and might even be thought to be obvious, at least to those
of a general empiricist persuasion (as Kant is in these matters).

It is not, however, the view with which Kant is normally
credited, and the reason is clear. Kant's words in the *Prolegomena* suggest a certain picture of how perception is related
to experience: judgements of perception are somehow en-
capsulated in the temporally later judgements of experience, so
that what begin as purely perceptual items are later given a 'new
reference' to objects. This picture is reinforced when we recognise, as I suggested earlier, Kant's tendency to look 'through'
the judgement to the structure of experience to which it relates:
the one kind of experience is 'contained' in the other. The difficulty that some philosophers find in this picture, however, is not
that it is dubious psychology. It is rather that, when suitably
upgraded into a logical thesis, what it presents us with is the
doctrine that judgements claiming objective validity can be
formed, if at all, only from a basis of judgements of perception
whose objects seem to be those minimal ones of immediate
sensory awareness – impressions, ideas, representations as items
of inner sense, sense data – call them what you will. Judgements
claiming objective validity, in short, are logically posterior to the
class of subjectively valid judgements. The seemingly innocuous
claim about the evidential basis of objectively valid judgements
in perception is turned into the special empiricist thesis about
the primacy of immediate sense awareness in claims to know
matters of fact, a thesis that notoriously leads to scepticism.

If this is the correct way to construe the *Prolegomena* distinction, the basic difficulty in it is already apparent: the main argument of the first Critique is against any such logical relationship as that which it suggests. In the *Critique of Pure Reason* Kant emphatically does not believe that the public world, or any judgement about it, is constructed out of experiences having purely private references. The burden of the Transcendental Analytic is that judgements about one's immediate perceptual experience make sense only as logically dependent upon judgements about an objective world of things and events in space and time, and not as being prior to or a foundation for them. The *Prolegomena* distinction as it is normally interpreted thus runs counter to Kant's central claim as it is found in the second edition of the Critique: the condition of the possibility of experience is that at least some of it should be of an objective world.

On my 'innocuous' version, however, it need not follow that judgements of perception are prior to judgements of experience in the sense that the latter are somehow *derived from* the former. If that were Kant's contention then it would have to be rejected. The way in which judgements of experience 'are first' judgements of perception could at best be the way in which every empirical judgement which makes a knowledge claim must relate to something given in perception. But this does not mean that the judgement of experience states that it is so given – judgements that simply state how something is given to perception are in Kant's terminology merely judgements of perception, subjectively valid and incapable of embodying knowledge claims.

Nevertheless, even on the most charitable reading of the *Prolegomena*, there still remains a formidable problem. In the second edition of the *Critique of Pure Reason*, and explicitly for instance at B 141–2, all *judgements* are said to claim objectivity, so that there can be no judgement which is not a knowledge claim:

> But if I investigate more precisely the relation of the given modes of knowledge in any judgement, and distinguish it, as belonging to the understanding, from the relation according to laws of the reproductive imagination, which has only subjective validity, I find that a judgement is nothing but the manner in which given modes of knowledge are brought to the objective unity of apperception. This is what is

intended by the copula 'is'. It is employed to distinguish the objective unity of given representations from the subjective.

That feature which, in the *Prolegomena*, is said to be a peculiar characteristic of judgements of experience only, namely objective validity, is in the final version of the Critique apparently made a defining feature of judgements in general. So if the Transcendental Deduction tries to show that categories must be involved in all knowledge claims, and every judgement must aspire to be such a claim, the idea of a judgement that is merely subjectively valid must go. When Kant wishes to contrast the objective validity of knowledge claims with something that is merely subjective, the latter is usually spoken of as mere association of ideas. There may be a problem in the first Critique as to how this distinction gets *expressed*, but the distinction is there, and the *Prolegomena* distinction does not fit it. The difficulty is not a merely terminological one that can be evaded by grafting the *Prolegomena* contrast on to the Critique, that is by maintaining that only judgements of experience employ categories and make knowledge claims that possess objective validity while allowing judgements of perception still as a useful contrast. According to the Metaphysical Deduction *any* assertion simply by virtue of its having a logical form carries with it an associated category or categories, and so if judgements of perception are judgements at all then they too must presuppose categorial distinctions. By the criteria of the *Prolegomena* that ought to make them candidates for objective validity. Judgements of perception, it seems, must either not be merely subjectively valid or not be judgements at all.

The arguments, however, are not all on the side of the first Critique, though some commentators have thought so. Kemp Smith, for instance, says that the distinction in the *Prolegomena* 'is entirely worthless and can only serve to mislead the reader. It cuts at the root of Kant's critical teaching', and 'the illegitimacy and thoroughly misleading character of this distinction hardly require to be pointed out'.[6] A more recent commentator, Jonathan Bennett,[7] finds that Kant handles the distinction 'very sloppily', and though this is not as such to say the distinction is illegitimate, he does think that it is put to objectionable use in the first Critique; or perhaps it would be better to say he thinks it is not put to any use at all there, since Kant 'tacitly restricts the meaning of "judgement" to that of "judgement of experience"'. Curiously enough, it is just that restriction, which Bennett finds 'arbitrary and illegitimate', that in Kemp Smith's view saves the Critique account from the 'worthless' distinction of the *Prolegomena*: 'in the section before us [i.e. B 140–2] there is no trace of it. The opposition is no longer between subjective and objective judgement, but only between association of ideas and judgement which as such is always objective'. Thus whilst Kemp Smith thinks the Critique view is the only coherent one, Bennett, it seems, tends in the other direction.

W. H. Walsh[8] is inclined to agree with Kemp Smith that the *Prolegomena* distinction is an aberration, although he thinks it is a philosophically interesting one. Stephan Körner,[9] on the other hand, works the distinction unhesitatingly into his outline of Kant's mature view on empirical judgements. His presentation of Kant's arguments for the necessity of the categories needs the contrast between 'a perceptual or subjective empirical judgement' and 'an objective empirical judgement'. Using this contrast Körner can show how Kant progresses from a position roughly identifiable with classical empiricism to the insights of the Transcendental Deduction. For the objectivity claim of judgements of experience is seen as identical with the objectivity claim which the Transcendental Deduction seeks to justify. Thus Körner adopts the *Prolegomena* position precisely in order to clarify Kant's justification of the categories, which are not involved in purely perceptual judgements. P. F. Strawson,[10] too, places the distinction between the subjective and the objective in experience at the heart of his reconstruction of the Deduction: it is essentially involved in his defence of the claim that the possibility of self-ascription of experiences on the part of the subject requires that we should be able to distinguish between a subjective stream of experiences and an experienced objective world of things and events. Something like the *Prolegomena* contrast seems tailor-made for articulating the distinctions on which Strawson's argument rests.

It is possible, then, to argue that the first Critique *needs* something like the doctrine of the *Prolegomena* to sustain its central argument, or, if not precisely that, that the first Critique has to come to terms with that doctrine. One cannot ignore it as a mere aberration. When so much that concerns the formulation of Kantian claims in the first Critique is unsatisfactory, we cannot afford to neglect a distinction that *prima facie* is promising.

There are a number of directions in which we might turn to make the distinction more acceptable and salvage what seems important in Kant's designation of judgements of perception as subjectively valid judgements. We might (*a*) retreat from the idea that they are *judgements* and regard them simply as personal avowals and declarations. Or we might (*b*) continue to think of them as judgements but retreat from the idea that they are valid only for the subject making them. Both courses are fraught with difficulties but also raise some interesting issues.

Walsh[11] has several things to say pertinent to alternative (*a*). He assumes that in the *Prolegomena* Kant wishes to distinguish within experience between the merely subjective in perception, that is, 'how things seem to me', and the objective recognition of 'how things are'. Now Kant describes judgements of perception as connecting two or more perceptions in one subject after the manner of Hume's psychological association of ideas; and he describes judgements of experience as connecting perceptions through the application of the categories, so making them judgements about objects. What is needed then is a characterisation of those private and personal judgements about how things seem that will go some way towards meeting Kant's apparent reluctance in the first Critique to call them 'judgements'. If we take the class of utterances known as 'personal avowals' to conform roughly to Kant's judgements of perception, a way seems open. For personal avowals, at least according to one interpretation, are not properly to be spoken of as judgements at all, although they express what occurs in a subject's consciousness, and are in that sense subjective and 'private to him'. It is a familiar claim that such utterances are incorrigible – that we cannot be mistaken in what we say. But it might also be said, appealing to the principle 'if you cannot be wrong you cannot be right either', which Wittgenstein made much use of, that personal avowals cannot properly be described as judgements at all if it is thought to be essential to judgements that questions of verification can arise with respect to them.

Walsh, however, takes the view that personal avowals are neither unambiguously subjective nor unambiguously judgements. What view of them we take will depend on what inferences we believe them to license. If, for instance, Smith's saying 'I feel cold' is taken to permit others merely to say that Smith *says* he feels cold, then the utterance 'I feel cold' (as said by Smith) is not a judgement but an avowal proper or 'a mere declaration'. It does not state something that is a fact for everybody, and judgements, whatever else may be true of them, purport to state facts. Such an utterance, Walsh says, 'would fall short of judgement and so, however appropriate, possess neither objective nor subjective validity'. On the other hand, if Smith's saying the words 'I feel cold' is taken to permit others to say not merely that Smith *says* he feels cold but 'Smith feels cold', the utterance can qualify as a judgement: something is claimed as a fact that is a fact not for Smith only but for everyone. It is a truth about the world, namely that a certain person feels cold. Walsh suggests that Kant's so-called judgements of perception as declarations of what is going on in us 'hover between avowals and judgements proper', since there is no clear indication of what we are supposed to take them to license. The trouble here, however, is not that Kant's so-called judgements of perception indeterminately license one or other of Walsh's inferences, but that Walsh does not offer us a genuine alternative. It must be a mistake, I think, to say that when 'I feel cold' is taken as a personal avowal all that is permitted in the way of inference is that the speaker *says* that he feels cold. At least on one way of construing avowals *that* someone says 'I feel cold' is itself a reason for thinking that he does, though *his* utterance is not something which is either verified or falsified by him. The utterance 'I feel cold' can be said to be true or false only in a special sense, for its truth coincides with its truthfulness. So someone can justify his belief that Smith feels cold on the grounds that Smith says he does, because Smith is not a liar. If Wittgenstein is to be believed, someone can hold that this is true of personal avowals without holding at the same time that 'I feel cold' is a judgement that describes a state of affairs albeit a subjective one. If that is right, the trouble with Walsh's alternatives is not that it is unclear which of them Kant's judgements of perception license, but that when construed as personal avowals they seem to license both. To that extent, although we may retreat from the idea that judgements of perception are judgements in the direc-

tion of treating them as personal avowals, it would nevertheless
not be true of them that they were valid for the subject only.

The Wittgensteinian approach to declarations of feeling or
mental states is, of course, controversial, but we might in any
case feel that what we wish to say about them is not to be extended
to everything that comes under Kant's heading of 'judgements
of perception'. Whatever may be the case with declarations of
feeling or emotion, we must surely resist the assimilation to
them of what, in the philosophical tradition, have been relegated
to the status of sensations – that is perceptions of the sensory
qualities of objects. Indeed, just because there is this difference
the relevance of personal avowals to Kant's discussion of judgements of perception seems somewhat slight. So rather than
explore this line of country further we may fall back on alternative (*b*) mentioned earlier: judgements of perception are judgements, but they are not valid only for the subject making them.

What we concentrate on here, as Walsh suggests, is the contrast between 'it seems' and 'it is'. There is a familiar argument
that judgements of perception, when taken to be judgements
about what figures in a subject's immediate perceptual awareness, are viable only in contrast to Kant's more general class of
judgements of experience: statements about how things seem to
be presuppose the possibility of statements about how things
are. On this view if a judgement of perception describes what
appears in perceptual awareness, then the judgement that that
is how something appears entails nothing about how it actually
is; nevertheless it could not function as a statement about what
is 'merely apparent' except by contrast with possible statements
about what experienced things really are like. Kant's own
examples of judgements of perception seem to bear this out:
they mention public objects without actually making positive
attributions to them; the concepts of such objects simply would
not be available if these judgements of perception were logically
prior to experiential judgements about these objects. This, of
course, merely serves to underline the point noted earlier that
in the logical order of things judgements of perception cannot
be what serve as the basic data for knowledge about the world
from which one moves on to judgements involving categorial
application. Judgements of perception have a function *within*
the scheme of judgements that have objective validity and not

outside it.

This discussion then of the *Prolegomena* passage must, so far, be an inconclusive one. Kant's way of making the distinction in terms of a contrast between judgements having merely subjective and judgements having objective validity does not match his general claims about what is involved in empirical knowledge, and in any case the kind of judgements that fall under his title 'judgements of perception' are by no means homogeneous. Even if we concede that alternative (*a*) lends some support to a non-judgemental avowal interpretation of some of Kant's candidates for judgements of perception (a suggestion I questioned anyway), this interpretation is implausible for many of those utterances that Kant characterises as judgements of perception, namely those that do seem to concern the perceived qualities of objects though only as private impressions. This latter kind of judgement suggests alternative (*b*), since the familiar contrast between what seems and what is the case appears to preserve the judgement character at least of those judgements of perception that are convertible into judgements of experience, but again only if it is also granted that there is no logical progression from the former to the latter.

But in what sense, then, are we to say that judgements of perception thought of in this way have only subjective validity? Statements about what is in one's immediate awareness, whether these concern one's feelings or immediate sense-impressions, may be true only of the subject who has these feelings or impressions, but this does not make them valid only for the subject. The contrast between the merely subjective and the objective cannot be identified with that between subjective and objective validity. It has to be made in some other way. For this we turn to the *Critique of Judgement*.

(IV)

Subjective Validity in the Critique of Aesthetic Judgement. The *Critique of Judgement* takes a distinction between subjective and objective validity for granted and puts it to extensive use. The contrast now, though, is less between judgements of perception and judgements of experience than between subjectively valid *aesthetic* judgements and objectively valid *cognitive* judgements.

Yet there are two strands in the Critique of Aesthetic Judgement which, in the light of the *Prolegomena*, may contribute to an understanding of the role of subjective validity in Kant's scheme. The first strand can be found in Kant's distinction between objective and subjective sensation; the second, running through the entire Critique of Aesthetic Judgement and especially prominent in the first Introduction to it, makes use of the distinction between two directions of reference – to an object and to a subject.

The two strands meet in this passage:

> When a modification of the feeling of pleasure or displeasure is termed sensation, this expression is given quite a different meaning to that which it bears when I call the representation of a thing (through sense as a receptivity pertaining to the faculty of knowledge) sensation. For in the latter case the representation is referred to the Object, but in the former it is referred solely to the Subject and is not available for any cognition, not even for that by which the Subject *cognizes* itself.

> Now in the above definition the word sensation is used to denote an objective representation of sense; and, to avoid continually running the risk of misinterpretation, we shall call that which must always remain purely subjective, and is absolutely incapable of forming a representation of an object, by the familiar name of feeling. The green colour of the meadows belongs to *objective* sensation, as the perception of an object of sense; but its agreeableness to subjective sensation, by which no object is represented: i.e. to feeling, through which the object is regarded as an object of delight (which involves no cognition of the object). (§ 3, 206)

Such a passage should make us at least pause before asserting that Kant abandoned the *Prolegomena* distinction. Three years after the second edition of the first Critique he seems still to have a use for the subjective/objective contrast as relevant to a distinction between different kinds of judgement in terms of their validity. It is true that he does not in § 3 specifically distinguish between two kinds of judgement; the distinction is rather between two kinds of representation, although these are elsewhere clearly thought of as giving rise to two kinds of judgement.

In terms of what I have called the first strand, the second paragraph in particular offers a way of looking once more at the *Prolegomena* position that preserves its spirit if not its letter. In place of a distinction between those judgements of perception that can and those that cannot be the basis for objective judgement, we are offered a distinction between objective and subjective sensation (*Empfindung*). Just as some judgements of perception, according to the *Prolegomena*, can but need not be converted into judgements of experience, so, according to the text we are now considering, some representations which Kant here calls 'sensations' can, but need not, become the basis for information about the world – the external world as well as our own inner states. These sensations are 'objective' sensations. And as the *Prolegomena* distinction maintained that some judgements of perception remain irremediably subjective, so the later passage speaks of those sensations (*Empfindungen*) that can never figure in knowledge claims as 'subjective' sensation or 'feeling' (*Gefühl*).

This is Kant's way of bringing into operation a distinction that his empiricist predecessors found so intractable precisely because they were committed to the view that all perceptions are 'on the same footing' (to quote Hume) as they appear in the mind, thus making problematic that reference to things which is characteristic of some of these perceptions. Kant, by contrast, makes reference to objects or lack of it constitutive of his distinction between perceptions of inner and outer sense, and he can do so by presupposing the argument of the first Critique in general and the Transcendental Analytic in particular. So he is in a position to say, without qualms about the justification for saying it, that 'we shall call that which must always remain purely subjective, and is absolutely incapable of forming a representation of an object, by the familiar name of feeling', and separate what is thus purely subjective from 'objective' sensations – even though in one respect these sensations too are private to the percipient. In terms of Kant's example 'the grass is green', the basis for this judgement is indeed a sensation, but an objective one, and the judgement can lay claim to objective validity: it tells us something about an object having certain qualities. The judgements 'the green of the grass is agreeable' and 'the green grass is beautiful', on the other hand, as mentioning subjective sensation or feeling, have only subjective validity

and claim nothing about the object's qualities. They are not, in
that sense, about the grass but about the speaker and his feeling
something when he has certain experiences.[12] Subjective sensations, we must suppose, share with objective ones the character
of being items in awareness. But as feelings of the subject they
indicate how the subject is affected rather than how the object
which affects the subject is qualified. All this appears already in
§ 1 of the Analytic of the Beautiful, where Kant presents the
feeling of pleasure or displeasure as an exception to a general
rule about sensations:

> Every reference of representations is capable of being ob-
> jective, even that of sensations. . . . The one exception to
> this is the feeling of pleasure or displeasure. This denotes
> nothing in the object, but is a feeling which the Subject has
> of itself and of the manner in which it is affected by the
> representation. (203/204)

Presumably because these exceptions, that is feelings, yield
no information and thus cannot lead to knowledge claims, they
do not figure in the analysis of the *Critique of Pure Reason*. In
that work Kant concentrates entirely on the presuppositions of
empirical *knowledge*, and to knowledge claims and their justification subjective feelings are clearly irrelevant. In terms of the
distinction between subjective and objective, only that which
can be given an objective reference is material for a critique of
knowledge. We may therefore conjecture that this is the reason
for the predominance of objectivity claims in the first Critique,
which, as we have seen, can make one wonder whether objective
validity allows of any contrast at all. In the *Critique of Pure
Reason* Kant does not pursue the possibility of a contrast and,
as we have seen, at times proceeds as if he ruled it out altogether.
In the more comprehensive mood of the *Prolegomena*, however,
a context wider than that is briefly envisaged, which leads to the
distinction we have discussed at length. The objective side of
the distinction alone receives detailed attention in the *Prolegomena*; the problem of subjectivity, of subjective validity and
of the feeling content of experience had to wait for the third
Critique. Only here does Kant begin to map out the territory
that had been neglected. Seen from the standpoint of the
Critique of Judgement, the *Prolegomena* distinction – however
muddled in its formulation – can therefore serve to focus atten-

tion on something that is central to an understanding of the judgement of taste, namely a differentiation among the representations of inner sense that enables us to say that a certain kind of judgement can be in one sense *about* an object without making an epistemological claim.

Even in the first Critique, however, we can find some indication that the contrast between objective and subjective validity was already present in Kant's thinking. In a condensed and difficult passage of the Transcendental Aesthetic (B 44/A 28–9), tucked away in a general remark on the nature of space, he distinguishes in this way between sensation and feeling: there are 'subjective representations, referring to something *outer*', as for example sensations of colours, sounds and heat, which are correlated with the senses of sight, hearing and touch; and there are the sensations of taste which, though also 'subjective representations', do *not* refer to 'something outer' and thus correspond to the 'subjective sensations' or 'feelings' of the *Critique of Judgement*. In the passage in the *Critique of Pure Reason* Kant's use of the term 'subjective' seems to conflate several aspects that I have been trying to separate. When Kant speaks of 'subjective representations referring to something outer', as for instance sensations of colour, sound and heat, the required sense of 'subjective' is that in which a judgement may simply record the having of a certain sensation (e.g. 'I have a sensation of red') as opposed to a judgement which attributes a property to an object (e.g. 'the tower is red'). A judgement may be subjective in this sense even if it concerns sensations that have reference to something outer, and indeed may be our sole reason for attributing a property to an object. On the other hand there are, Kant thinks, representations that not only do not, but could not, refer to something outer, and these are subjective not merely in the sense of being contents of awareness, but also precisely in the sense of being incapable of having an outer reference: the representations of taste are in this position. 'The taste of wine does not belong to the objective determinations of the wine' but rather to 'the special constitution of a sense in the subject that tastes it' (A 28). Unlike the judgement 'the tower is red', which, although based on a subjective representation, can nevertheless form the ground for attributing a property to an object, 'this wine tastes sour' refers to what the subject feels when sensing.

Feeling (*Gefühl*), Kant says, is 'an effect of sensation' (A 29), and no object can be characterised by it. Although this is an isolated passage that Kant does not develop further in the first Critique, it is easy to read it as foreshadowing the later distinction in the Critique of Aesthetic Judgement between objective and subjective sensation. The distinction between sensed and felt awareness may also once again be taken as a critical comment on the failure of empiricist thought – as evidenced by the stock-in-trade arguments for the relativity of perception – to distinguish between, for example, 'this is warm' and 'this tastes nasty'. The former statement can be given an objective correlative, the latter can not. It may be that Kant himself had no clear, or no clearly consistent, position in his epistemology as to whether there are primary and secondary (or tertiary) qualities, but at least by the time he wrote the *Critique of Judgement*, and perhaps before, he had worked out a distinction between judgements having objective and those having subjective validity to which any distinction between primary and secondary qualities would be irrelevant.

I began this section by noting a shift in the Critique of Aesthetic Judgement away from the *Prolegomena* contrast between judgements of perception and judgements of experience to one between judgements expressive of feeling and judgements of matter of fact or empirical judgements, mediated by a distinction between subjective and objective sensations. The *Prolegomena* problem of how there can be *judgements* of perception becomes the problem of how there can be *aesthetic* judgements of taste. What we now have is the claim that these are judgements based not on those sensations that can be called 'objective' because they are sensations capable of 'referring to something outer' (in the language of the first Critique passage), but on those that are now more felicitously called 'feelings': no objects can be characterised by the attribution of these to a subject. Aesthetic judgements thus have a special position amongst those judgements that earlier on, in the *Prolegomena*, Kant described as subjectively valid: they must remain outside the range of even potentially cognitive concern with objects. In this respect they correspond to those judgements of perception that cannot be converted into judgements of experience.

Among the aesthetic judgements that Kant singles out for

special attention the judgement of taste (*Geschmacksurteil*), also called an aesthetic judgement of reflection, alone requires justification by transcendental argument.[13] Judgements on the agreeable, aesthetic judgements of sense (which are the other kind of aesthetic judgement) appear in the main only for purposes of comparison with the judgement of taste. Both kinds of aesthetic judgement are said to be subjectively valid since in neither does the object figure as an object of cognition; only the judgement of taste, however, lays claim to universal assent. In this sort of judgement the object figures as an object of delight. But the response to the object when we find it beautiful is not the result of perceiving a quality in it that is causally responsible for our perceiving it in that way, as the sensible properties of objects are responsible for our perceiving for example colours and sounds. It is this peculiarity of the aesthetic judgement that Kant wishes to capture by calling it a subjectively valid judgement. Feelings and not sensations are the 'representations' that give rise to it.

We now have already in view the second strand to be found in the Critique of Aesthetic Judgement, namely the emphasis on the two different directions of reference in a judgement. The 'direction of reference' does not seem to have much to do with the ostensible form of a judgement. Certainly when Kant speaks (in § 3) of an 'objective sensation' in the case of a representation that is 'referred to an object', the suggestion must be that a judgement based on such experience is objectively valid because an ascription is made to an object that is the logical subject of that judgement. But the judgement 'this frieze is beautiful' also has the ostensible form of 'this frieze is colourful', and yet it is a judgement in which the representation 'is referred solely to the Subject' (§ 3, 206). This might suggest a distinction between the ostensible form of a judgement and its true logical form, but the evidence in the third Critique does not point unambiguously in this direction. Judgements of taste, Kant affirms, have the logical form of singular judgements; moreover, a judgement of the form 'x is beautiful' can be the basis for a generalisation, that is to say, for a 'logically universal judgement'. Thus the judgement 'this frieze is beautiful', as a judgement made by me or others on a number of different occasions and on different individual objects, may suggest a generalisation 'friezes are beautiful'. Although a generalisation of particular aesthetic judgements, this one is not, Kant emphasises, itself an aesthetic judgement but must count as logical. Logical form then, it seems, is not going to be any sure guide to the kind of judgements aesthetic judgements of taste are.

More to the point, perhaps, is the function of the predicate in such judgements. That is to say, the conditions of application of empirical predicates (or concepts) are such that what the object is like determines whether the predicate is true or false of the object. In the case of the predicate 'is beautiful', however, what determines its application is not simply what the object is like or what is observed to be empirically true of it. If that were the case, then whether an object was beautiful or not would be something that could be 'read off' from the observed properties of the object. But this is not so. Rather, what determines whether the predicate applies in a judgement of taste is a particular response of delight consequent upon the subject's contemplation of the object. The reference in an aesthetic judgement is, in this sense, to the subject.

Part of the drift of my earlier remarks has already been to suggest that the pre-categorial nature claimed by Kant in the *Prolegomena* for his 'judgements of perception' cannot possibly be defended. The non-categorial nature of aesthetic judgements cannot be defended either. Fortunately, in the Critique of Aesthetic Judgement Kant seems to have forgotten or laid aside his earlier distinction in terms of absence or presence of categories, and in this respect his later position is a vast improvement on the description of subjectively valid judgements in the *Prolegomena*. If it is the direction of reference that makes the difference between objective and subjective validity rather than the involvement or non-involvement of categories, some of the puzzlement created by the *Prolegomena* distinction has already been removed.

We can extend to aesthetic judgements the idea that judgements of perception involve categories without, I believe, endangering Kant's characteristic theses about aesthetic judgements. As pointed out already, these judgements are singular judgements and simply by virtue of that fact must involve categories. What is distinctive about them in contrast to other judgements of sense perception is that the categories play no *justificatory* role in assessing their validity or invalidity. For while categories are supposed to underpin the application of empirical concepts to objects, this is not a *determining* feature of the validity of an aesthetic judgement. Every judgement is, in Kantian terms, a unification of representations. It orders what is given in experience and links the expressions that stand for representations, whether of sense or not, by the copula 'is'. Judging *qua* unifying is thus always a function of the understanding that cannot but make use of concepts. No concepts of any kind, however, are thinkable without the logically prior 'pure concepts of the understanding', the categories. So if judging is an operation of the understanding, then subjectively valid judgements cannot be exceptions on *that* score. If aesthetic judgements of taste 'unify representations' as all judgements do, then concepts cannot be totally absent.

Notoriously, Kant overstates his case here, to the extent of saying that concept application plays *no* role in aesthetic judgement. But in saying that the judgement 'this is beautiful' does not apply a concept or concepts to experience, what we should stress is merely that there is no rule for the application of a concept in terms of which the truth of 'this is beautiful' can be intersubjectively established. Aesthetic judgements of taste, we might say, do employ concepts but not in the way that judgements of experience do. The concept of beauty and its associates are not descriptive. The peculiarity of the application of concepts in the making of aesthetic judgements is that when they apply they do so because of something in the individual's awareness of the object, his feeling toward it. Only subjects can feel pleasure or displeasure, and judgements appraising something on the basis of felt apprehension thus differ radically from judgements made on the basis of cognising something about the object sensed. Aesthetic judgements refer feelings to a subject as their 'determining ground'; descriptive empirical judgements take the objective turn by referring sense representations to an object as 'determining ground'.

Kant's insistence on the non-cognitive character of aesthetic judgements and, associated with this, their non-conceptualising character, has led some commentators to say that aesthetic judgements cannot be about objects at all. But we can acknowledge, as Kant says, that feeling 'must always remain purely subjective, and is absolutely incapable of forming a representation of an object' (§ 3, 206) while still allowing that feelings are about something, namely an object. That this is not a way of being aware of the features or qualities of something – as seeing is, for example – does not put it outside the range of normal experience that presupposes the categories. Although pleasure in an object is not as such cognition of it, it is still open to us to say that without some mode of awareness that does not preclude cognition we should not have the feeling of pleasure. We are not forced to the conclusion that an object can be an object of delight only if it is not an object of cognition: an aesthetic judgement may be about an object that is also an object available for description. It is just that in appraising the object *aesthetically* we make no epistemological claim.

Kant's devoting of the entire first part of the *Critique of Judgement* to the exploration of problems connected with aesthetic judgements as in an important sense *sui generis* must be read against the background of his having already worked out his position in respect of knowledge claims and the arguments essential to their formulation. Without this contrast the Critique of Aesthetic Judgement could not have got under way. What the third Critique adds cannot therefore be wholly divorced from Kant's epistemology. On the contrary, it needs that doctrine in order to show that knowledge claims, important as they are, are not everything we can express in judgement form about our experience of living in a knowable world.

3

Aesthetic Appraisals

(I)

In his aesthetic inquiries Kant assumes that there are aesthetic judgements with features peculiarly their own and then asks for the necessary presuppositions of their possibility. This is a characteristically Kantian approach. Given that something is the case he asks 'What makes it possible?' The inquiry thus becomes a transcendental one. So, given the special characteristics of aesthetic appraisals, he asks what must hold if their having these characteristics is to be intelligible. Kant's answer to this question in the first part of the *Critique of Judgement* is notoriously problematic. To assess it we need to know first what the special characteristics of aesthetic judgements are supposed to be. This task might well loom at least as large as the transcendental inquiry into the presuppositions of their possibility. There seems plenty of room for disagreement before we can even raise the transcendental question. In the interest of pressing on with it I propose therefore to accept Kant's characterisation of the judgements in question for the time being, hoping that in investigating their presuppositions we shall become clearer about what the conceptual features are that he is ascribing to aesthetic appraisals as he sees them.[1]

The most prominent features of judgements of taste – or aesthetic appraisals – which Kant singles out are (*a*) that they are in a certain sense subjective, and (*b*) that, nevertheless, anyone who appraises an object aesthetically lays claim to the consensus of others. If this is right, and if we can say not only what must hold for this to be so, but also that the presuppositions involved are coherent and make sense, then we have at least an account of judging aesthetically that avoids pure subjectivism on the one hand and pure objectivism on the other. Of course that we can give a coherent account along Kantian lines – *if* we can do so – is no proof that it is the correct and only account of what we are doing when we appraise something aesthetically. But as one of the main difficulties readers find with Kant's text concerns the justification of ascribing (*a*) and (*b*) jointly to aesthetic appraisals, clarifying how Kant argues may help us towards an assessment of the account he gives.

This said, however, another doubt becomes insistent. For even if we suspend judgement on the conceptual features that Kant attributes to aesthetic judgements and follow him in the search for the presuppositions of judgements having those features, it might be said that the results are too meagre, perhaps even trivial, to provide a plausible account of how aesthetic appraisals are possible. For the argument has mainly appeared to Kant's commentators to be simply this: the necessary presupposition of any subjective judgement which nevertheless is deemed to be universally valid is just that the endowment with capacities for experiencing and for knowing is something we all have in common. Now apart from any reservations we might have as regards merely stating a psychological fact about human beings, we should wonder whether this could possibly serve as an adequate expression of what must be true if aesthetic appraisals are to have the characteristics that Kant claims for them. A lot depends here on the account he can give of the relevance to aesthetic appraisals of the 'faculty' doctrine.[2] If we were clear on this point perhaps it would just be obvious – as it apparently was to Kant – that the claim to general assent in judgements of taste was adequately grounded by that account. Even if we were not clear on this, we might at least be in a better position to say what further steps were required.

These two themes, then, namely the nature of those conceptual features Kant ascribes to aesthetic appraisals and the presuppositions of appraisals having those features are the topic of this discussion.

There is no easy way into the *Critique of Judgement*. No help is to be gained from the famous Kantian architectonic, which in the case of this Critique seems to have got out of hand entirely. Nor is either the first or the second Introduction to the work an illuminating guide to what is to come. In addition a commentator on any aspect of it will have to decide whether to regard the work as a whole, in which case the Critique of Teleological Judgement may have important implications for one's reading of the Critique of Aesthetic Judgement; or whether to adopt an approach of a more piecemeal character, taking the first half of the Critique to stand on its own for conceptual issues connected with aesthetics and epistemology, without commitment to Kant's welding together of aesthetics and teleology in the interest of 'bridging the gap' between nature and morality. For reasons that may become clearer as I go on, I am in favour of the piecemeal approach.

The third Critique is afflicted even more than the other two Critiques by Kant's tendency to conflate arguments about conceptual features and their presuppositions with phenomenological descriptions of the working of the human mind. Not only are the latter as such often of doubtful validity; they fit very uneasily, if at all, into the kind of investigation Kant is explicitly conducting. In what follows I shall try to keep these two strands apart and emphasise readings that play down the descriptive psychology in favour of the logical implications of what he says. Defeat will have to be admitted at times when what Kant actually says cannot be reconciled with what one would like him to have said. I shall have to be content with showing that at least some key arguments in this dense thicket can be made intelligible when careful attention is paid to the various legitimate and illegitimate moves he makes from one strand to the other.

(II)

Subjectivity. Judgements of taste, or aesthetic appraisals as I shall call them – judgements ascribing beauty to something – are, according to Kant, *subjective*. In § 1 of the First Moment of the Analytic of the Beautiful he says:

> The judgement of taste, therefore, is not a cognitive judgement, and so not logical, but is aesthetic – which means that it is one whose determining ground *cannot be other than* subjective. (203)

Here we have, to begin with, a negative characterisation of aesthetic appraisals: they are not cognitive judgements. To say this is to say, with Kant, that 'we do not refer the representation of it to the Object by means of understanding with a view to cognition'. So we are not here concerned with the kind of judge-

ment whose necessary presuppositions it was the task of the
Critique of Pure Reason to elucidate. But this does not mean that
we can disregard what was there elucidated: on the contrary,
the contrast with cognitive judgements and their presuppositions is central to the argument of the Critique of Aesthetic
Judgement.

Empirical, informative judgements are characterised in
general by the way in which they bring objects under concepts
so as to provide knowledge of a world independent of ourselves
and our perceptions. For such judgements criteria of significance and of truth are relatively unproblematic because we can
rely on perceptual experience providing that which, when conceptually sorted, is in principle recognisable and repeatable.
Empirical judgements employ concepts of objects that embody
or presuppose in their rules of application certain necessary
conditions specifying the features that must hold if there is to
be a public world for us to experience. Descriptions of the world,
or rather of something in the world, are possible only if our
experiences are relatable in ways that for Kant amount to 'falling
under concepts'. To say that aesthetic appraisals are 'subjective'
is, in its negative aspect, simply to say that they are not judgements bringing objects under concepts for the end of cognition.
Aesthetic appraisals in Kant's theory make no epistemological
claims.[3]

This denial carries with it some positive implications. Since
statements about sensations or immediate experiences are often
described as 'subjective' in one sense of this slippery term it is
tempting to assimilate aesthetic appraisals to that class of judgements. But Kant clearly does not want to liken aesthetic
appraisals in their subjectivity to judgements about sensations,
for the latter may indeed qualify as 'objective' in Kant's sense
of this term:

> Every reference of representations is capable of being ob-
> jective, even that of sensations (in which case it signifies the
> real in an empirical representation). (§ 1, 203)

This remark is interesting not only for what it says about sensation. If every reference to sensation is capable of being objective
this tells against all interpretations of Kant – and there are many
such – which insist that aesthetic appraisals are concerned with
'immediate experience', and then support this assertion by

arguing that because aesthetic appraisals are not 'cognitive' in the sense just outlined the *objects* of such judgements cannot be identical with objects that *can* be the occasion of an objective judgement. But it does not follow from the fact that aesthetic appraisals are not objective that that towards which they are directed cannot be the same as that about which objective judgements are possible. The appeal to sensations in immediate awareness fails to support the difference between subjective and objective judgements, since sensations, despite their immediacy and dependence on an experiencing subject, may well be 'brought under concepts' in judgements which would then count as objective. For this reason alone – and there are others that could be adduced, as Kant in fact does when he separates sensuous gratification from aesthetic experience proper – we cannot understand the subjectivity of aesthetic appraisals by connecting them simply with sense-contents of immediate experience.

One mode of consciousness, however, which the argument of the *Critique of Pure Reason* does not fit into its scheme, and which has to be distinguished from sensation, is the feeling of pleasure or displeasure. This feeling, Kant says, 'denotes nothing in the object, but is a feeling which the Subject has of itself and of the manner in which it is affected by the representation' (§ 1, 204) We have to distinguish between, say, my consciousness of the Acropolis when I make a perceptual claim about it and my consciousness of the same building when I take delight in my perception of it. For in aesthetic judgement, 'if we wish to discern whether anything is beautiful or not, we do not refer the representation of it to the Object by means of understanding with a view to cognition, but by means of the imagination (acting perhaps in conjunction with understanding) we refer the representation to the Subject and its feeling of pleasure or displeasure' (§ 1, 203).

Positively, then, aesthetic appraisals are judgements that involve consciousness of pleasure or displeasure in the experience of an object. Moreover, Kant wishes to draw a fundamental contrast between perception of an object that involves conceptualisation, and delight in the awareness of an object that is not a perceptual act, although it can no doubt be significantly related to one or more such acts:

> . . . the judgement of taste is not a cognitive judgement . . .
> and hence, also, is not *grounded* on concepts, nor yet
> *intentionally directed* to them. (§ 5, 209)

A perceptual act involves as part of its description an epistemological claim. This does not hold, in Kant's view, for the delight
basic to a judgement of taste – although it would be hard to
maintain that without a perception and at least the possibility
of an epistemological claim associated with it there could be an
object of delight. Whether, nevertheless, Kant denies this I shall
consider later in connection with his attitude towards existence
claims in respect of aesthetic objects.

A distinction that is important here for Kant's discussion of
aesthetic pleasure is that which he makes between sensation and
feeling. Pleasure is a feeling, not a sensation in the sense in
which according to Kant sensations may be 'objective', that is,
falling within the range of what the *Critique of Pure Reason*
covers in respect of the necessary presuppositions of empirical
thought and experience. Feelings, apparently, are not objective
in that way, and this is why Kant also speaks of objective and
subjective sensations as an alternative to talking of sensation
and feeling. The distinction is discussed in the First Moment
in connection with the agreeable and that which gratifies our
senses. Kant's formula here is: '*That is* AGREEABLE *which the
senses find pleasing in sensation.*' (§ 3, 205). Clearly this is open
to misunderstanding if the ambiguity both of 'sensation' and of
'pleasure' and 'pleasing' is not borne in mind. In one sense
'sensation' covers what we might call the sensed contents in the
experience of objects; in another it can also refer to feeling. But
feeling is not a mode of awareness of objects as sensation in the
first sense is. Rather it is a state of the subject who has experiences. Feeling 'must always remain purely subjective, and is
absolutely incapable of forming a representation of an object'
(§ 3, 206). In terms of this distinction sensation of the green
colour of the grass in a meadow is 'objective', the agreeable
feeling which we might have when we see the meadow is 'subjective': objective sensation is a mode of awareness of objects,
subjective sensation is the feeling I have or may have when some
object is an object of my sensation in the first sense. Granting
the distinction we still have to recognise that feelings may be
directed towards something: although pleasure is not a mode of

awareness of objects, an object may nevertheless be that towards which pleasure is directed. The agreeableness of the green colour of a meadow belongs to 'subjective sensation' 'by which no object is represented: i.e. to feeling, through which the object is regarded as an Object of delight' (§ 3, 206). With the logical distinction between subjective and objective sensation goes an epistemological one: subjective sensation, unlike objective sensation, 'is not available for any cognition, not even for that by which the Subject *cognizes* itself' (§ 3, 206). That is to say, through feeling we do not gain knowledge of anything, not even of ourselves who have these feelings. The feeling through which an object becomes an object of delight involves 'no cognition of the object' – or subject.

It does not, however, follow from this distinction, as some have thought, that the connection between feeling and cognition is completely severed. Certainly, that feeling in the sense of 'subjective sensation' cannot be a source of cognition is a clear consequence of the way in which Kant introduces the notion. But even if we accept the distinction as valid this still leaves it open to us to say that without some mode of awareness either involving cognition or having the potential for it we should not have a feeling of delight. To say that an object can be an object of delight *only* if it is not at the same time, or some other time, an object of cognitive awareness seems altogether too restrictive. This is relevant to the question whether, and if so, how, concepts are involved in aesthetic appraisals.

The distinction of objective and subjective sensation, or of sensation and feeling, helps at least in this respect: it is now somewhat clearer why Kant might have thought that something left out of the other two Critiques, but especially the first, deserved full consideration in an additional Critique, that is, consideration in the transcendental manner. For whilst the first Critique can certainly cope – and has to do so – with sensation in so far as there are conditions for its objectivity, sensation in the other sense of subjective sensation of pleasure or delight is not so catered for. But if to speak of 'subjective' sensations is not to speak of personally idiosyncratic or arbitrary responses to the experience of an object, then we must be able to give some account of the conditions attaching to the 'feeling' kind of response. It might be thought that this task ought to form part of a wider inquiry into the place of subjective sensation generally in our conceptual scheme; or, if not that, then it ought to be made clear why merely sensuous gratification, in contrast to delight proper to aesthetic appraisal, is not suitable material for such an inquiry. Kant, however, is interested in sensuous gratification only in contrast to aesthetic pleasure in order to bring out the force of arguments which, whilst acknowledging fully the subjectivity of aesthetic appraisals, attempt to show that such judgements nevertheless have an aspect so importantly analogous to 'objective' judgements that *a priori* conditions must be involved. This is the aspect of their alleged universal validity. Before turning to that, however, it is worth dwelling a little on the contrast just mentioned between sensuous gratification and the delight proper to judgements of taste.

A feature of Kant's argument that puzzles many commentators is the apparently explicit assertion that a judgement of taste rooted in pleasure or displeasure is – in contrast to a judgement upon the agreeable – indifferent to the 'real existence' of the object of the appraisal. This seems to remove all object-centred perceptual immediacy from aesthetic appraisals; it also seems contrary to my suggestion that an object about which perceptual claims involved in objective judgements may be made may also be the object of aesthetic delight.

Now Kant certainly holds that when delight is delight in the *existence* of something this does not count as pure aesthetic delight. The reason is that directedness towards existence implies *interest* in that which exists. That is to say, pleasure in an object where the existence of the object is the *vital* element arises necessarily either directly or indirectly from some desire or want in respect of that object. This, however, is not what is involved in a judgement of taste and, apparently, *cannot* be involved in any genuine aesthetic appraisal:

> Now, where the question is whether something is beautiful, we do not want to know, whether we, or anyone else, are, or even could be, concerned in the real existence of the thing, but rather what estimate we form of it on mere contemplation. (§ 2, 204)

It would be a mistake, I think, to infer from this that no object related to our aesthetic experiences of pleasure or displeasure need exist. As Kant says:

> *All one wants to know* is whether the mere representation of
> the object is to my liking, no matter how indifferent I may
> be to the real existence of the object of this representation.
> (§ 2, 205, my italics)

Is 'indifferent to the real existence' the same then as 'whether
the object exists or not' ? In one sense – and the sense with which
Kant is obviously not concerned here – it must be true that we
are *not* indifferent to the existence of things we take delight in –
even if we phrase this more carefully as 'in the awareness of
which we take delight'. But such interest, in the sense of concern
for that which gives us this special pleasure, can at best be a consequence of the delight we feel, and not a constituent part of it.
We may, of course, feel an overpowering sense of gratitude that
the Acropolis still exists. The question is whether Kant wishes
to deny even consequential interest. A footnote suggests that he
does: 'But, of themselves, judgements of taste do not even set
up any interest whatsoever.' (§ 2, 205). The phrase to note here,
however, is 'of themselves'. Aesthetic appraisals are complete
before they lead to interest. Indeed, any interest aroused, Kant
admits, has strong connections with the 'cultural milieu' in
which we find ourselves; but it is neither part of nor ground for
the appraisal. It is obviously the kind of interest that would be
more valuable in a civilised society if it followed upon an aesthetic
appraisal and did not just come about by considerations of
prudence (e.g. the collection of art works as an investment where
we certainly care for their 'real existence', or wanting to preserve
the Acropolis in the interest of the tourist trade). Kant's throw-
away remark on the 'cultural milieu' might be taken to point to
a feature of the concept of art in which Kant was not explicitly
interested but which is now much discussed: that what we
historically expect of art works is part of the value we place on
their existence, continuity and preservation. Since the Renais-
sance at least, and until comparatively recently, our concept of
art has involved the notion of something that survives not only
its maker but also any individual appraisals. An age that might
grow accustomed to art for immediate disposal, for being used
up in the act, so to speak, would have different expectations and
perhaps no longer provide that 'cultural milieu' in which subsequent interest in the existence of the object could be even
extrinsically related to aesthetic appraisals.

If, then, we interpret 'indifference to real existence' as meaning that there is no 'factor of dependence' in the sense of want, need, or desire for the object that produces or enters constitutively into the appraisal, we have said no more than what Kant says in the latter part of this passage:

> It is quite plain that in order to say that the object *is beautiful*, and to show that I have taste, everything turns on the meaning which I can give to this representation, and not on any factor which makes me dependent on the real existence of the object. (§ 2, 205)

But the earlier part of this passage is open to more than one interpretation – that is, 'everything turns on the meaning which I can give to this representation'.

One interpretation would be this. Whether I judge something to be beautiful or not turns on whether the feeling of delight occurs irrespective of whether any object is actually experienced. Aesthetic judgements are then possible even when in reality there exists no object for the judgement to be about, provided I can give a 'meaning to the representation' that can stand without reference to the existence of the object. It is a short step to argue from this that since delight must be delight in something, whether or not an object really exists, the object of delight must be something else, such as a phenomenal appearance. Robert L. Zimmermann,[4] for example, attributes this view to Kant:

> If I am concerned with the beauty of something I am necessarily unconcerned about the existence of that something, I am concerned only with the manner in which it impresses me. My experience of it is not bound to the existence of it so that if it did not exist and was an illusion my judgement concerning its aesthetic quality would not be altered. The only condition is that I be impressed and have a representation.

'Having a representation' is here obviously not taken to exclude illusions, dream images and 'mere imaginings'.

Another interpretation, and one to which I subscribe, says merely that an aesthetic appraisal depends on a reaction to experience of the object where the response does not take the form it does because the existence of the object is desirable or desired for some reason or other.

(III)

Conceptualisation and General Validity. So far I have emphasised
that aspect of Kant's argument in which he maintains that to
predicate beauty of an object is not to make an epistemological
claim. Aesthetic appraisals are not *grounded upon* concepts, and
we can add here: not grounded upon concepts of objects in the
sense of the *Critique of Pure Reason*. This means that they cannot
be established in the way that ordinary epistemological judgements can be, namely by reference to whether an object *is* characterised in the way that those judgements say it is. Appraisals
do not characterise the object by ascription nor do they entail
descriptions of an object. What, then, are they about? They are
concerned, Kant says, with delight in an object consequent
upon 'the mere estimate of its form'. It might be said that, if this
is so, we ought to be able to justify them by reference to an
object's formal characteristics – balance, design, arrangement of
parts, and so on. But the citing of these characteristics alone
would not amount to justifying an aesthetic appraisal, for
aesthetic appraisals do not assert that objects have such properties. Rather, they indicate delight consequent upon awareness of an object seen in that way.

There still remains for Kant, then, the problem of accounting
for the second feature of aesthetic appraisals mentioned earlier:
that anyone who appraises an object aesthetically supposes himself to be judging it on behalf of all other persons. Kant emphasises many times that the claim to universality cannot rest on
empirical generalisations about the delight which people might
feel in the experience of form. Indeed he insists that even if a
person diverged in his judgement from everyone else he would
still be supposing his judgement made on behalf of all others –
and he would be right to do so: this supposition is not empirically
based but something conceptually required by aesthetic
appraisals.

Kant's resolution of the tension here between the claims of
subjectivity and universal assent involves a complex inter-
weaving of the latter claim with various theses about the role of
conceptualisation, or lack of it, in aesthetic appraisal. In a way,
Kant uses his position on the role of conceptualisation as a kind
of shock effect, for it appears at first that what he claims is not

only incompatible with the possibility of universal assent but even contradicts it. In a series of complicated moves, however, he tries to turn the apparent contradiction into mutual support. How, we might wonder, can judgements which in Kant's opinion do not bring 'objects under concepts' nevertheless claim universal assent – something which is comparatively easy to show for judgements that have objective validity, that is are intersubjectively verifiable? The universal validity claim seems *prima facie* unjustifiable in appraisals which Kant himself characterises as subjective. If we are to make sense of his attempt to show that the claim is not misguided, but is actually a necessary feature of judgements of taste, we need to clarify the nature of the relationship between the claim to *subjective* universal validity in aesthetic appraisals and the conceptualisation of experience.

Kant argues for the claim to universal assent partly in terms of what our practice in aesthetic appraisal is (§ 7), partly in terms of a general inference from the non-idiosyncratic nature of aesthetic appraisals (§ 6). In the latter case the argument is this. Suppose that a certain object is an object of disinterested pleasure to A. Then A will have no reason to believe that his pleasure arises from personal inclinations, desires, needs, and so on, which may be peculiar to him; idiosyncrasies are ruled out in the case of pleasure properly called aesthetic. It follows that whatever grounds or reasons there might be for the pleasure A takes in the object he must think of these as grounds or reasons why others also should take similar pleasure in the object:

> Hence he must regard it [the delight] as resting on what he may also presuppose in every other person; and therefore he must believe that he has reason for demanding a similar delight from every one. (§ 6, 211)

It might be said here that in so far as Kant presents us with an argument for the claim to universal assent as a *necessary* feature of aesthetic appraisals this argument is only as strong as the inference from 'there is no reason to suppose my judgement of taste to be idiosyncratic' to 'there is reason to believe that my judgement of taste can claim validity for everybody'. In fact, however, the general argument of the Critique of Aesthetic Judgement does not give explicit support to this inference. Kant seems to think that in showing the grounds or reasons why *in general* a person finds disinterested pleasure in the contemplation of an object he has *ipso facto* shown why this pleasure must be universally communicable or of general subjective validity. This is what the so-called Deduction is about:

> How is a judgement possible which, going merely upon the individual's *own* feeling of pleasure in an object independent of the concept of it, estimates this as a pleasure attached to the representation of the same Object *in every other individual*, and does so *a priori*, i.e. without being allowed to wait and see if other people will be of the same mind? (§ 36, 288)

When we turn to the material Kant assembles for an answer to this question, however, the story, far from turning into a transcendental one, seems in danger of degenerating into bad psychology.

Consider the problematic linkages Kant makes between

(1) the distinction between subjective and objective;
(2) the claim to general validity;
(3) epistemological judgements which bring objects under concepts and aesthetic judgements which do not;
(4) characteristic activities of the judging subject when forming epistemological judgements.

Despite the contrast in (3), (2) is said to hold for both epistemological and aesthetic judgements; and the contrast in (3) is associated with the distinction in (1) between subjective and objective – indeed, it is in terms of the contrast in (3) that Kant first introduces the subjective/objective distinction. But under the stress of his obsession with putting points in terms of his famous 'faculties of the mind' the subjective also becomes associated with (4), that is with the mind's contribution in forming epistemological judgements about experience. This then becomes the basis for maintaining that judgements of taste have indeed a claim to general validity, but only to subjective general validity. Implied in this move, though not explicitly stated, must be that epistemological judgements also claim subjective general validity, something that is of no special significance for them and tends to be taken for granted because it is objective validity that makes them the judgements they are.

Kant, then, seems to be arguing in this way. In epistemological judgements the mind is characteristically engaged in activities that bring objects under concepts; this is what confers objectivity on such judgements. If we think of this activity as the subject's contribution to experience then aesthetic judgements, while not bringing objects under concepts, must nevertheless include some mental activities characteristic of the subject's activity in judging, and it is this that allows us to extend the claim to general validity to judgements of taste, but only as subjective general validity.

This unpromising sketch of an argument hardly receives much clarification when we investigate the characteristic activities mentioned in it. It is in this context that Kant introduces the notion of imagination and understanding as working 'in harness' in epistemological judgements and as being in 'free play' in aesthetic judgements. He cites imagination 'for bringing together the manifold of intuition', and understanding 'for the unity of the concept uniting the representations' (§ 9, 217). In epistemological judgements imagination plays the role of holding together the disparate items given in awareness long enough (metaphorically speaking) for the understanding to subsume the particular givens under concepts. Thus in epistemological judgements imagination is tied down to the role of serving understanding in its task; it has a necessary function but one subordinate to the purposes and ends of the understanding. Aesthetic judgements, by contrast – and staying still within Kant's faculty language – are similar to epistemological judgements in that the same mental faculties are involved, but they are involved differently. Imagination is said not to be in the service of the understanding, but 'free'. The understanding has not dropped out of the picture but is 'in balance' or in 'free play' with the imagination. It is this 'free play' of the faculties in judgements of taste that has somehow to form the background to the claim to general validity of aesthetic appraisals, albeit only a subjective validity.

So much for Kant's account in terms of what Gilbert Ryle has happily called 'feudal allegory'.[5] It is possible to see in it, perhaps, the general thrust of the argument. Aesthetic judgements do not conceptualise experience but must bear some relation to conceptualisation, or at least to its possibility, if there is to be any foundation for the claim to general validity. For the paradigm of such validity is the judgement of experience that brings objects under concepts. Now since judgements of taste are not objective in the paradigmatic sense, but subjective only, the necessary relationship must be found in what is *required for* conceptualisation. If we talk in terms of mental faculties what conceptualisation requires is understanding and imagination working 'in harness'. But if we talk *merely* in terms of faculties it is difficult to see how imagination and understanding are involved in non-epistemological judgements in such a way as to provide grounds for the claim to general validity. Kant at times seems to think that this follows simply from noting that the same faculties are involved as those needed for the formation of objective judgements of experience. But before we can even begin to consider whether this is so we need answers to at least two questions. First, what role do imagination and understanding play in aesthetic appraisal? And secondly, how does it follow from the fact that both are involved in epistemological judgements as well as in aesthetic appraisals that the latter can lay claim to general validity, if only of a subjective kind? That is, if the role of imagination and understanding 'in harness' in epistemological claims is not the role of these faculties in aesthetic appraisals, what is it? The metaphorical answer is that they are in 'free play', but this has as yet no definite content, for it is used simply to contrast with the way in which these two faculties are supposed to function in the making of epistemological claims, that is 'in harness' – another metaphor.

Here it seems imperative to disengage the statements of transcendental requirements from their psychological overtones. In terms of the former we have first to note that it is a feature of aesthetic appraisals, according to Kant, that they do claim universal assent without being objective judgements in the sense of the *Critique of Pure Reason*. This presupposes, however, that features necessary for the conceptualisation of experience reappear in aesthetic appraisals, that is to say, some at least of the presuppositions of empirical discourse must reappear as the presuppositions also of aesthetic appraisals. If this is too strong a claim a less strong one may be substituted: the possibility of aesthetic discourse must be shown to rest on the possibility of empirical discourse, for nothing else would underpin the claim to general assent that is a central feature of aesthetic appraisal. So the difference in the claims to objective and subjective validity respectively will have to be shown by finding a

difference in the deployment of these presuppositions.
These are, or seem to be, the transcendental requirements.
But they are associated in a baffling way with Kant's psychology.
It is one thing to claim that judgements of the understanding,
conceptualising experience, are related to aesthetic appraisals
in their presuppositions; it is another to describe the mental
state of someone who makes aesthetic appraisals in terms of these
presuppositions. Yet the latter is what Kant seems to be doing
when he says, for example:

> Hence the mental state in this representation [in judge-
> ments of taste] must be one of *a feeling of the free play* of the
> powers of representation in a given representation for a
> cognition in general. (§ 9, 217, my italics)

That Kant should say *this* is possible only because he describes
necessary presuppositions in terms of mental functioning – in
this case the interplay of imagination and understanding. But
we have to ask: how can the feeling of delight in situations of
aesthetic appraisals derive from a conceptual condition of
making them?

Kant's own answer here compounds the difficulty, for he
specifically says that the claim to general assent in aesthetic
appraisals must rest on *consciousness* of the requirements for
knowledge which are the same for everybody:

> for we are conscious that this subjective relation [between
> imagination and understanding] suitable for a cognition
> in general must be just as valid for every one, and conse-
> quently as universally communicable, as is any determinate
> cognition, which always rests upon that relation as its sub-
> jective condition. (§ 9, 218)

Here we have a quite explicit conflation of talk about conceptual
presuppositions or conditions of aesthetic appraisals with
phenomenological descriptions of what goes on in the mind of
the person making such appraisals. This conflation has consequences for the status of aesthetic pleasure and displeasure in
Kant's account. For it seems that he has now brought about a
change in how we should think of the pleasure involved in
aesthetic appraisals. Earlier on he had settled the question of
logical precedence in respect of the subjective estimate of form
or the feeling of pleasure or displeasure in favour of the former.
The feeling of pleasure could not have precedence since we

should then be deprived of a basis for the claim to general assent. Whatever affords the grounds for universal validity must be what has precedence in aesthetic appraisal. Pleasure then, we might agree, must be a consequence of our appraising something in which pleasure is taken, and we might expect that Kant would produce as the object of aesthetic pleasure that which is judged to be beautiful. We have seen, however, that this runs into difficulties since we have to distinguish aesthetic appraisals from judgements of objects of experience. It is true that *one* difficulty here may be more apparent than real. That is to say, when Kant makes the required distinction on the grounds that an aesthetic appraisal is directed not so much to the object apprehended as to the state of awareness with which an object is apprehended, I claimed on his behalf that this does not commit us to the view that no object is therefore the topic of appraisal. What we are committed to is rather that whatever features the object has *qua* object, as possible topics of epistemological claims, do not enter constitutively into the aesthetic appraisal of it.

Nevertheless, even if we can clear up one source of misunderstanding in this way, a problem remains. For if the task now becomes one of showing how appraisals so characterised can still be intersubjectively valid, the way in which this is to be done is apparently by connecting aesthetic appraisals and cognitive judgements through their conceptual presuppositions. Those passages where Kant talks about the conditions of making either sort of judgement bear this out. Yet because of the involvement of conceptual presuppositions with apparent descriptions of mental states, by the time he has introduced the crucial notion of the 'free play' of imagination and understanding, the phrase 'object of aesthetic appraisal' has acquired a disconcerting ambiguity. That is to say, Kant now seems to think of the object of pleasure not as an object that could also be the object of cognitive judgements but rather as a mental state, the state namely in which imagination and understanding are in 'free play'.

Going even further than this Kant seems at times, when he connects the resultant pleasure with the claim to general assent, to be arguing that the pleasure arises because we become aware of something that all people possess, namely cognitive capacities, and that we feel pleasure in the mere ability to share our own mental states with others (cf. § 9, 218). But whilst this may well be so as a matter of fact it could not provide an argument for what Kant is trying to show, namely that the pleasure felt in aesthetic appraisal is claimed from others as a matter of necessity and does not come about because we enjoy shared or shareable experiences by virtue of, say, our natural disposition toward a social life. Indeed, that he does not think this is made clear on a number of occasions. For instance, 'empirical judgements do not afford any foundation for a concept of the necessity of these judgements' (§ 18, 237) – that is aesthetic appraisals which claim general assent as a matter of necessity. Even if we can discount passages like the one just mentioned (§ 9, 218) in which Kant speaks as though the pleasure involved in the ability to share one's feelings or states of mind is to be identified with aesthetic pleasure, it must be admitted, I think, that the connection between the 'harmony of the faculties' and aesthetic pleasure is only fitfully brought out. In general Kant seems to think of them as the same thing, so that there is aesthetic pleasure in an object in that the experience of the object involves harmonious play of imagination and understanding, and it is this harmony that is supposed to be universally communicable.

Although it is difficult to find anything in Kant that is not somehow affected by this conflation of presuppositional and speculative-psychological arguments, at least an outline of a logical argument is, I think, discernible. In the final section I shall attempt to say what I take this to be.

(IV)

In the Deduction of Pure Aesthetic Judgements Kant says of the claim 'this flower is beautiful' that it is 'tantamount to repeating its own proper claim to the delight of every one', and then continues:

> Now what else are we to suppose from this than that its beauty is to be taken for a property of the flower itself which does not adapt itself to the diversity of heads and the individual senses of the multitude, but to which they must adapt themselves, if they are going to pass judgement upon it. And yet this is not the way the matter stands. For the judgement of taste consists precisely in a thing being called

> beautiful solely in respect of that quality in which it adapts
> itself to our mode of taking it in. (§ 32, 282)

So whilst we expect a judgement of experience to be checkable against what is the case, in aesthetic appraisals this is not so. Here, whether a judgement of taste is correct depends on the conforming of the object in experience to possible ways of experiencing it. It depends on the object's adapting itself to our mode of awareness, not on our adapting our judgement to what is objectively the case. Judgements of taste record pleasure consequent upon the estimate of form in the object; but that objects exhibit pure form is not a fact about objects. Rather, that they have pure form is a consequence of our being able to have certain kinds of experience of them, of our being able to see them in certain ways. This must be one source of Kant's conviction that in aesthetic appraisals we do not bring objects under concepts. For if we did this it would mean that the criteria of concept application would be independent of the way in which things are experienced. But for Kant it is a striking feature of aesthetic appraisals that the mode in which something is experienced determines what the object is experienced *as*, that is as beautiful form. Nevertheless, when it is said that aesthetic pleasure is a consequence of estimates of form this implies also that such appraisals are not arbitrary. On the contrary they necessarily lay claim to general assent. The question then arises: how can the non-arbitrary character of aesthetic appraisals be reconciled with their subjectivity, that is with 'a thing being called beautiful solely in respect of that quality in which it adapts itself to our mode of taking it in'?

Here we can use, in summary form, some of the results gained in section 11 above. The judgements with which to contrast aesthetic appraisals are, we saw, in the first instance those we make about things and situations in the world, objective judgements about matters of fact. For such empirical and informative judgements *a priori* conditions can be shown along the lines of Kant's arguments in the first Critique. Descriptions of something in the world, assertions of something holding good as a matter of fact, are possible only if our perceptual experiences are relatable in ways of which Kant speaks as 'falling under concepts'. Reformulating the demands of the Transcendental Deduction we might say: epistemological judgements are pos-

sible on condition that (*a*) what is given in experience can be
identified in a spatio-temporal world, and (*b*) both sortal concepts (categories) and descriptive concepts are applicable to
what is given. The resultant judgements have objective validity
in the sense that criteria for verification and falsification are in
principle available.

In *this* sense what is judged in aesthetic appraisals does not
'fall under concepts'. Now clearly the contrast here cannot be
simply that empirical judgements employ concepts and aesthetic
appraisals do not. The contrast must lie in whether the objects
are or are not brought under concepts in the sense just outlined.
That which is judged to be such-and-such is said to fall under
concepts because certain necessary conditions restrict the application of these concepts to what can be picked out with their aid.
'Falling under concepts' is therefore a phrase we should reserve
for the application of concepts to non-conceptual givens. For
Kant this is both pragmatically and theoretically the most basic
mode of judging: pragmatically, because we primarily want to
know and to be able to say what is the case and what counts as
evidence for or against our knowledge claims; theoretically,
because it is standard-setting for all judgements. Only if other
kinds of judgement can be shown to stand in some logical relation to judging what is the case, only if the conditions of other
judgements can be related to the conditions of empirical discourse, can we begin to entertain criteria of validity distinct
from those we employ in objective judgements. That epistemological judgements are standard-setting for Kant can hardly be
in doubt, although he puts the reason for their priority in terms
of the working of the human mind. But at least implicit in his
talk of the 'free play' of the cognitive faculties in aesthetic judgements is the logical point that aesthetic appraisals are possible
only if empirical judgements are possible.[6]

There are two related aspects to Kant's claim about aesthetic
appraisals involving the 'free play' of the cognitive powers.
Negatively, the characterisation of what is presupposed by
aesthetic appraisals is made in terms of a *contrast* with empirical
judgements. The restrictions built into the application of
empirical concepts, that is the restrictions operative in empirical
predication which guarantee verifiability, are *not* operative in
aesthetic appraisals. In this sense such appraisals are 'free', that

is free from the conditions under which empirical judgements work in so far as they are judgements of matter of fact. Put in Kant's language, imagination in aesthetic judgements must be 'considered in its freedom', in contrast to the way in which imagination figures in empirical judgements where it signifies the recognitional element in the conceptualisation of experience. 'Imagination considered in its freedom' can be read as stressing the independence of aesthetic appraisals from the rules and criteria that are conditions for the objective validity of empirical judgements. Kant, it is true, is inclined to see this independence as a sort of prising loose of one mental activity – employment of the imagination – from the ends and purposes of another – employment of the understanding – so that they stand in 'free play'. But the overall argument, whatever a detailed exposition may import into it, surely yields a logical point: the full conditions of objective knowledge claims must be recognised as *not* holding in aesthetic appraisals.

Yet although such appraisals escape the restrictions necessary to the application of empirical object concepts it is just because these restrictions hold in the empirical context that aesthetic judgements can be recognised as *not* committed to them. Aesthetic appraisals are intelligible only against the background of epistemological claims and rules of application of concepts to objects. In saying this we have moved over to the positive aspect of Kant's thesis. If aesthetic judgements are in one way logically independent of empirical judgements they are also in some sense logically dependent. In terms of the roles assigned to imagination and understanding in aesthetic appraisals, imagination is said not only to be 'free' (the negative point), but to stand in 'free conformity to law':

> Taste, then, as a subjective power of judgement, contains a principle of subsumption, not of intuitions under *concepts*, but of the *faculty* of intuitions or presentations, i.e. of the imagination, under the faculty of concepts, i.e. the understanding, so far as the former *in its freedom* accords with the latter *in its conformity to laws*. (§ 35, 287)

The principle of subsumption referred to here must be seen, I believe, as indicating the kind of dependence of aesthetic appraisals on empirical judgements that I have just suggested is involved in Kant's account. It is only in the context of judgements that apply concepts of the object to experience that we can conceive of a kind of perceptual judgement whose criteria of correctness concern not the conformity of the experience to the object, but of the object to the experience – the kind of judgement in fact that Kant calls judgements of taste and I have discussed as aesthetic appraisals.

That aesthetic appraisals, in so far as they are 'estimates of form', are logically dependent on empirical judgements can be expressed nowadays in terms of claims about the alleged relationship between aesthetic and non-aesthetic properties, even if the exact nature of the connection continues to elude us.[7] Indeed, in the absence of formal relations of entailment between the possession by an object of aesthetic properties and possession by the same object of non-aesthetic or natural properties, the notion of presupposition may well seem fitted to capture the weaker logical relationship that is thought to hold between aesthetic and non-aesthetic properties. Kant's argument, however, concerns not the way particular estimates of form are related to particular empirical judgements, but rather the dependence of one sort of discourse on another for its possibility. That this dependence exists, it might be thought, ought indeed to follow simply from what I have described as the standard-setting role of empirical judgements, for it was the argument of the first Critique that *their* possibility was demanded if we were to make coherent sense of experience at all. Judgements of taste, though not judgements about objects of experience, are experiential judgements. They must be parasitic upon those experiential judgements that are non-aesthetic.

Yet though this is part, and perhaps the most important part, of Kant's thesis, it is not the whole of it, for what this dependence does not bring out is the peculiar relationship that must exist between one kind of experiential judgement – aesthetic appraisals – and another – epistemological judgements – both considered as subject to whatever conditions hold for the making of any judgement of experience whatever. The trouble here is that Kant's account of these conditions, where it does not simply stress the logical dependence we have already noted, steers us, it seems, in a direction no one really wants to go – namely in the direction of the Schematism chapter of the first Critique. It is there that Kant at his most obscure seems to give us relevant hints. But we might well, echoing Parmenides, want to say: 'From this inquiry keep your thoughts far off'. All would depend on whether we could find anything illuminating in Kant's dense remarks in Schematism on the relationship of understanding and imagination in *all* kinds of experiential judgements. That task cannot be undertaken here. One question, though, should be raised. Granted that in the perception of form we do not fill in what we see in terms of concepts of the object – for perception of form is not a case of perceptual recognition of objects as being of this or that kind – and granted that the capacity to perceive form in objects is nevertheless an exercise of that same capacity operative in the perceptual recognition of non-aesthetic properties of objects, can the logical relationship between aesthetic appraisals and epistemological claims yield a justification for the claim to general assent made by aesthetic appraisals ? Kant seems to believe that it does.

The answer, I think, is already implicit in what has been said so far. Epistemological judgements have a standard-setting role, that is they presuppose conditions that must hold if we are to make coherent sense of experience, conditions which, as Kant puts it, are 'requisite for a possible experience generally'. Now whatever the outcome of an inquiry into the significance of the role of imagination and understanding in the *subjective* conditions of perceptual judgements in general will be, it seems that Kant must be pointing towards shared conditions that he expresses in pseudo-psychological terms of shared mental capacities. It does seem an ingredient in his view that implicit in the capacity to perceive objects is the capacity to perceive form. What we must avoid here is any suggestion that perception of form is more primitive in the sense that it arises at an earlier stage of the perceptual process that leads to the recognition of objects. This is the kind of suggestion Kant's references to the subjective conditions of all cognition in the Schematism chapter puts in our way. Whether the notion of temporal priority and some sort of primordial rooting of imagination in 'the depth of the human soul' (*Schematism*, B 180) can be translated into less objectionable logical terms is something only a close evaluation of the Schematism arguments could reveal. Supposing, however, that it could be done, we might then see how the argument supporting the claim for general assent in aesthetic appraisals could proceed.

Having noted that epistemological judgements are standard-setting in the sense of presupposing conditions that must hold generally of any experience we can make intelligible to ourselves, we now find that we have to associate the judgements arising from the experience of form with this claim, for the capacity to perceive form is tied to the capacity to perceive objects. We must therefore also extend to estimates of form this feature of experiential judgements about objects: if such estimates presuppose conditions that must hold generally for us to make coherent sense of experience, whatever these conditions may be, they must be conditions of *anyone's* experience for us to be able to talk about the experience of others at all. It is this that must form the justification of the claim for the possibility of agreement in aesthetic appraisals. It should be noted that what I have said just now does not simply repeat that the claim to universal assent is based on people being more or less alike in their experiential make-up – a claim we have already dismissed as too trivial to bear the weight of a transcendental argument for the *a priori* conditions of judgements of taste.

Perhaps we can now also see why – grotesque as this may sound to the exhausted reader of the *Critique of Judgement* – Kant found the Deduction of Pure Aesthetic Judgements so 'easy' (§ 38, 290). For once the capacity to perceive form is related to perceptual judgements of objects in the way here sketched, the standard-setting role of these judgements provides the grounds for possible universal assent in aesthetic appraisals without requiring us to establish the objectivity of such appraisals. Indeed trying to establish objectivity here would be the worst sin we could commit against those experiences that give rise to judgements of taste. For both the difficulty and the excitement in making aesthetic appraisals arise from our thinking of beauty *as if* it were a quality of objects. If it *were* so, straightforwardly, no one need bother about it or take delight in pointing it out. Subjectivity in aesthetic appraisal is not something to be overcome or eradicated: it is something that forms the basis of our common concern for intelligible appraisals that are not to be reduced to statements of matters of fact.

It is one thing, of course, to sketch a line of argument; quite another to make it fully intelligible, let alone plausible. What is clear, however, is that the *logical* basis of Kant's argument for the presuppositions that must lie behind and justify the two features of aesthetic appraisals with which I began – subjectivity and the claim to general assent – is a good deal more subtle and complex than it is generally credited with being. Although the argument provided here perhaps raises more problems than it solves, it raises them in a form which, I hope, is worth investigating. The problems with which it deals can be seen, when dissociated from the language of psychological mechanism, to lie at the centre of aesthetic theory.

4

Free and Dependent Beauty

(I)

What Kant has to say about *pulchritudo vaga* and *pulchritudo adhaerens* in the Third Moment of the Analytic of the Beautiful has not greatly recommended itself to his readers and critics. The distinction between 'free' and 'dependent' beauty seems intelligible enough at first sight, but the implications of making it in the way Kant does have been regarded for the most part with either bafflement or repugnance. It is argued by critics that the distinction leads to a trivialisation of aesthetics; that indeed if Kant were taken seriously, then wallpaper patterns and decorative friezes would have to rank higher in our aesthetic estimation than the Parthenon or Michelangelo's Sistine Ceiling. This, it is said, follows from Kant's assertion that only appraisals of 'free' beauty are *pure* judgements of taste, and from his selection of paradigmatic instances of such beauty: flowers (not considered as a botanical kind), humming birds (not considered *qua* birds), crustaceans, 'designs *à la grecque*, foliage for framework or on wallpapers, etc.' (§ 16, 229), and musical fantasias. All these, according to Kant, 'please freely and on their own account', they 'have no intrinsic meaning', 'represent nothing'. Only appraisals of such configurations are 'pure' judgements of taste. This, it is felt, is formalism at its most shallow extreme. In fact the only readers who have had something positive to say for Kant's distinction and his apparent higher ranking of free over dependent beauty are those who find in it an anticipation of, and critical foundation for, arguments asserting the primacy of abstract over figurative or representational art. In their view Kant prepared the way for modern formalism in the sense in which Clive Bell could say:

> Let no one imagine that representation is bad in itself; a realistic form may be as significant, in its place as part of

the design, as an abstract. But if a representative form has value, it is as form, not as representation. The representative element in a work of art may or may not be harmful; always it is irrelevant.[1]

Both the condemnation of Kant as too narrowly formalistic and the appraisal of him as a prophet of non-representational art rest principally on four claims:

(A) That he distinguishes free and dependent beauty in natural and artistic configurations.
(B) That the grounds for the distinction of two kinds of beauty are the same for nature and art.
(C) That judgements about free beauty are pure aesthetic judgements, judgements about dependent beauty impure.
(D) That what figures in pure judgements of taste is aesthetically preferable and more valuable than what figures in impure judgements of taste.

Claims A and C are clearly made by Kant. At the beginning of § 16 he says, substantiating claim A: 'There are two kinds of beauty: free beauty (*pulchritudo vaga*), or beauty which is merely dependent (*pulchritudo adhaerens*)'. And a little later in the same section claim C is brought out: 'In the estimate of a free beauty (according to mere form) we have the pure judgement of taste'. When a judgement is a judgement of dependent beauty, however, 'then it is no longer a free and pure judgement of taste'. If the distinction thus introduced is to work for nature and art alike, claim B or something like it is needed. Yet although there are grounds for thinking Kant makes this claim, the position turns out to be far from clear. Moreover, supposing we agree that the claim is Kant's, it is still difficult to see that the arguments he advances or sketches in support of it warrant its acceptance.

Claim D is obviously an interpretation of Kant rather than a claim explicitly made by him. It does not follow from claims A and C, which are admittedly his, nor from A, B and C together, assuming the truth of B, which is questionable in any case. So in D we have a highly controversial claim on the truth of which both the criticism of Kant as aridly formalistic and the praise of Kant as liberating aesthetics from the shackles of representationalism must ultimately rest. Yet this claim is not one we can without argument attribute to Kant: it is one that could emerge, if it emerged at all, only from a detailed investigation of his position. What such an investigation reveals is a much more complex situation than the simplistic view outlined at the beginning suggests. I shall try to unravel it in order to show at least that despite criticisms that may be levelled against claim B, we really have no right to attribute claim D to Kant. If this is so, we shall no longer have to say that he thought that wallpaper patterns are more beautiful than great paintings, or, in general, that form is aesthetically more valuable when it is pure rather than dependent for its beauty on conceptual and intellectual ties. To attribute the particular view to Kant is to say that he was aesthetically un-sophisticated to the point of simplemindedness. The general view raises a host of problems concerning the legitimacy of the central distinction between two kinds of beauty: to attribute it to Kant is to say that he was philosophically unsophisticated in not realising that such problems existed. I hope to show that Kant was neither aesthetically nor intellectually naive, although there is room for criticism of his position on other grounds.

Kant explicates the distinction between free beauty and beauty 'which is merely dependent' thus:

> The first presupposes no concept of what the object should be; the second does presuppose such a concept and, with it, an answering perfection of the object. Those of the first kind are said to be (self-subsisting) beauties of this thing or that thing; the other kind of beauty, being attached to a concept (conditioned beauty), is ascribed to Objects which come under the concept of a particular end. (§ 16, 229)

That is to say, the adjectives 'free' and 'dependent' are used to denote the absence or presence respectively of ties with a specific sort of concept, that is concepts involving the notion of an end. Exactly what this comes to will occupy us later. Here we may simply note that Kant links claim A immediately with C: as there are two kinds of beauty, so there are two kinds of judgements of taste, namely (*a*) judgements in which the ascription of beauty to an object is divorced from thinking of the object in terms of concepts involving the notion of an end or purpose, and (*b*) judgements in which such ascription is not so divorced. The first sort are pure, the second impure judgements of taste. Among the latter, the notion of perfection finds a place.

What is surprising is not that, having distinguished two kinds of beauty, Kant should make a distinction between two kinds of judgement, but that he should make a distinction between two kinds of judgement *of taste*. From what he has said so far in the first three Moments of the Analytic of the Beautiful we should expect the ascription of beauty in case (*b*) to be misguided and not a genuine judgement of taste at all. The idea that aesthetic appraisals of an object are connected with, or even based on, a concept of its end or purpose would seem to be a contradiction in terms (cf. § 15). Calling the second kind of judgement 'impure' makes no difference in this respect as it still is to count as a judgement of taste, an aesthetic appraisal. Any dilution of such a notion by admitting conceptual ties at all is a move away from the necessary conditions of aesthetic appraisals as outlined so far in the first three Moments.[2] Whether much or little is made of this apparent inconsistency in Kant's theory, it does establish that, in retracting the extreme claim of the non-involvement and irrelevance of *any* concepts in judgements of taste, Kant makes room for a type of judgement that is not to be assessed by the standards of pure aesthetic appraisals. If this is so, there is at least a *prima facie* doubt about the attribution of claim D to him in any straightforward way.

(II)

Free Beauty and the Pure Judgement of Taste. Kant elaborates the distinction between free and dependent beauty through a series of contrasts, with the result that discussion of one cannot easily be divorced from discussion of the other. Indeed pure judgements of taste are very often described and elaborated in terms of what they are not, namely impure judgements of taste. Nevertheless, I shall as far as possible reserve my remarks on dependent beauty for the next section since my primary concern now is with what I take to be a central problem of this whole discussion, that is, the relationship Kant sees between free beauty in nature and free beauty in art.

At the beginning of § 16, Kant elucidates the distinction between free and dependent beauty by means of examples. In judging a flower beautiful, he says, we take no account of its biological function as a reproductive organ of the plant and we therefore make a pure judgement of taste. This covers cases both

of being ignorant and of having sufficient knowledge of the biological function. In the first case ignorance of what a flower 'is
for' does not diminish the justification for passing an aesthetic
judgement on it; in the second case, even if there is knowledge
of the flower's biological purpose, this plays no part in appraising its beauty. Similar things may be said of Kant's other
examples – humming birds, birds of paradise, crustaceans. Of
course we may encounter special difficulties if we enlarge on
these similarities. For instance, while it is relatively easy to say
what flowers 'are for' botanically speaking, what humming birds
or crustaceans 'are for' is already problematic, presumably
requiring a wider context which is ecological rather than biological, with shades of teleological arguments just around the
corner. These special difficulties could be overcome, no doubt,
with sufficient care in specifying the natural ends and purposes
involved, whether of parts of organisms or of wholes in a wider
scheme, or of inanimate objects (Kant mentions crystals later
on) in the larger economy of nature.

These difficulties apart, we can say that an appraisal of a
natural object as beautiful counts as a pure judgement of taste
when the object is considered apart from any purpose it might
have in nature, whether this purpose is known or unknown to
us, and irrespective of whether such a purpose can be justifiably
attributed to the object, or is illegitimately read into nature as
part of a higher design. Whatever the ways in which natural
objects may be classified or categorised these are irrelevant to
an appraisal of free beauty. Such objects 'please freely and on
their own account'.

Now Kant immediately adds to the examples drawn from
nature those from art. This raises the expectation that here, too,
when we appraise something in a pure judgement of taste, all
considerations of ends or purposes with which the object may
be associated are in abeyance. The brevity of Kant's remarks,
however, obscures the complexity of the problems raised by this
transition from nature to art.

As examples of the freely beautiful in art, paradigmatic of
objects that are the topic of pure judgements of taste, Kant cites
– as we noted earlier – wallpaper and other purely decorative
patterns, and 'all music that is not set to words'. These objects
are said to qualify as objects of pure aesthetic appraisals because

'they represent nothing – no Object under a definite concept', and therefore are to be accounted freely beautiful. The question must arise, then, whether Kant wishes to give the same reasons or apply the same criteria for the ascription of pure beauty to natural and to man-made objects – whether, in other words, he makes claim B. For, at least *prima facie*, 'not falling under the concept of a particular end', which is offered as a criterion of free beauty in nature, and 'representing nothing', which is now introduced as the ground for ascribing free beauty to art objects, do not seem to be the same criterion. Does Kant then think that they are the same? It might be thought that he must do so if we believe that claim B holds. In the passage already quoted occurring at the beginning of § 16 Kant speaks in one breath of free beauty in nature and free beauty in art, jointly the objects of pure judgements of taste. But here the notion of representation does not appear. Instead the notion of what an object ought to be, the notion of perfection (or the absence of it) serves as a single distinguishing criterion linked with the concept of an end or purpose:

> The first [free beauty] presupposes no concept of what the object should be; the second [dependent beauty] does presuppose such a concept and, with it, an answering perfection of the object. Those of the first kind are said to be (self-subsisting) beauties of this or that thing; the other kind of beauty, being attached to a concept (conditioned beauty), is ascribed to Objects which come under the concept of a particular end.

How, if at all, do these various suggestions hang together?

If claim B is to stand, the identity of those conditions under which an object is to count as freely beautiful in nature and in art alike must be established; or, if not identity, a close logical relationship, or, to put it no higher, a close analogy. We do not get much help here from Kant's own formulations, which are thin on the ground and, where they occur, very compressed. We might, however, try a number of possible readings of what could be the relationship between the formulae 'presupposing no concept', 'not falling under the concept of a particular end', and 'representing nothing'. Schematically, four possibilities suggest themselves:

(1) The notion of 'representing nothing' could be seen as

somehow subordinate to the notion of 'not falling under the concept of an end'.

(2) Conversely, 'not falling under the concept of an end' could be seen as subordinate to 'representing nothing'.

(3) The two notions 'representing nothing' and 'not falling under the concept of an end' could be seen as differentiations within the general idea of 'presupposing no concept of what the object *should be*', applying to art and to nature respectively.

(4) 'Representing nothing' and 'not falling under the concept of an end' could be taken to be jointly implied by 'presupposing no concept of what the object should be', without any distinctive assignment of each of these two notions to the spheres of art and nature.

The first two possibilities may seem *prima facie* improbable for the very reason that they make no reference to the absence or presence of the notion of perfection ('what an object should be') that figures so prominently in Kant's account. For the same reason the last two possibilities appear more promising. Of all four it is true, I believe, that the notion of representation cannot bear the usual sense of 'portrayal' or 'depiction'.

It seems clear when we turn to interpretation (1) that we could think of 'representing nothing' as subordinate to 'not falling under the concept of an end' only if we gave up the idea that to represent something is to depict it. Then we could say, admittedly with some strain on our language, that 'not falling under the concept of an end or purpose' is the criterion we use in ascribing free beauty to nature or to art, but in the latter case 'not falling under concepts' is specified as 'representing nothing'. So that if x is a man-made object appraised in a pure judgement of taste, x does not represent anything in the sense of bringing whatever is perceived as its form under the concept of an end for which this form could be taken as a representation. If this were Kant's view, 'representing nothing' could be seen as a criterion for free beauty in art which is based on the general condition of 'not falling under the concept of an end'. But this works only if 'depiction' is not part of the meaning of 'representation'. It would hardly do to say that pure beauty in art is pure because the form of the thing does not depict any ends and purposes under which the object might be considered.

The first interpretation is not, then, one which would be

either easy or congenial to defend, although it must count as a possible if implausible account of Kant's statements in § 16, where examples are introduced with criteria for nature in terms of the absence of concepts of ends, and for art in terms of representing nothing. But if this first suggestion leads us to say odd things about freely beautiful objects in art its converse, interpretation (2), leads us to say even odder things about freely beautiful things in nature. For this second view would hold that the same condition is involved for both beauty in nature and beauty in art despite the discrepancy in Kant's formulation, because 'not falling under the concept of an end' could be understood as exemplifying for nature the general condition of 'representing nothing'. For instance, if we called a flower freely beautiful because considerations of its end do not enter into the pleasure derived from its form we should have to take this to mean that the flower does not appear to us as the reproductive organ of the plant and does not represent in its form the end or purpose of the flower. Again some sense could be made of this, given a little conceptual ingenuity, but only if 'representing' were divorced from 'depicting'. To say that a flower, when considered for its free beauty, is *ipso facto* not depicting its biological end or purpose would be nonsensical: nobody wants to say that flowers when considered as biologically functional depict their end.

So these first two suggestions are candidates for consideration only if the notion of representation is divorced from that of depicting. Yet it is just this sense of picturing that all adherents of the view that Kant anticipated attitudes towards non-figurative art must attribute to him.

We noted earlier that neither of the interpretations just sketched found a place for the crucial notion of 'not presupposing a concept of what the object should be'. The third interpretation, by contrast, does. For on this view we are to think of the idea of 'presupposing no concept of what the object should be' as differently exemplified in nature and art. The general condition holds for both with specific differences taken care of by differentiating between 'not falling under the concept of an end' (natural objects) and 'representing nothing' (art works). That is to say, judging something to be freely beautiful in nature is to disregard what the object could or should be, and this takes the form of disregarding its natural end or function; and judging something to be freely beautiful in art is to disregard what the object could or should be, and this takes the form of disregarding what it could or might be in its representational aspect. Beauty in nature is free when what the flower could be *seen as* is not part of the appraisal; beauty in art is free when what a man-made object could be *seen as representing* is disregarded.

Here we seem to have at last a plausible rendering of Kant's point, so obvious indeed that to labour it may appear pedantic. Nevertheless, I am not satisfied with it, and for a number of reasons. Clearly a lot more work would have to be done on relating the notions of 'falling under the concept of an end' and 'representing nothing' to the notion of perfection. It might be said that the notion of perfection has in any case a notoriously problematic role in Kant's scheme. This is so, but my difficulties lie in a rather different direction. In flowers, crustaceans, and other natural objects we are, so the suggestion runs, to disregard the biological, ecological, or even cosmological ends that these objects have; similarly, in art, for example wallpaper patterns, and so forth, we are to disregard what these patterns represent or that they represent – if, that is, they represent at all. This underlies the asymmetry between nature and art with respect to aesthetic appraisal rather more strongly than the attempt to bring them under the same general condition (i.e. 'not presupposing a concept of what the object ought to be') would allow. All the examples from nature that Kant cites, and presumably all those we could supply, have natural ends and purposes which, in the pure aesthetic judgement, can be disregarded. There is none which could not, if desired, be seen under the concept of an end. If what makes some natural objects, for example flowers, freely beautiful is connected with the particular attitude we take up towards them, involving the exclusion of ends or purposes, then there seems to be no reason why this should not hold for *all* natural objects. Now in man-made things the position is markedly different if we assume that the criterion of 'not representing anything' specified for art the idea of presupposing no concept of what the object ought to be, as 'not falling under the concept of an end' does for nature. It is certainly not the case that all human artefacts can be seen as representing something, so there can be no question of disregarding this feature of them in pure aesthetic appraisals. Of some art objects, notably of the kind Kant himself cites, it is true to say that disregarding their representational character cannot arise, simply because 'representation' in the sense in which it would be analogous to 'not falling under concepts of ends' in nature is not involved at all. In 'pure' music, for example, we do not have to suspend any representational ties in order to achieve a pure judgement of taste because there are none: in such cases, *only* the pure judgement of taste would be appropriate. So it seems that on the present interpretation nature presents a different picture from art. All natural objects could be seen as freely beautiful if we disregard their purposes, but none actually forces this attitude upon us. Among human artefacts, by contrast, there are some that seem to lend themselves *only* to pure aesthetic appraisals, whilst others might allow for both pure and impure judgements according to whether or not we disregard the representational aspect.

On interpretation (3), then, when Kant says 'there are two kinds of beauty' we should have to read this as elliptical for 'things can be appraised aesthetically in two ways', that is either by disregarding purpose and representation, or by paying attention to them in nature and art respectively. If this is so, however, much of what Kant says later on the beauty of man, for example, in analogy with the beauty of a building *qua* church, has to go. Both could be experienced and judged as freely *or* dependently beautiful. There is, on this view, nothing in flowers that makes them intrinsically freely beautiful, for they are, biologically speaking, no less under a particular concept of purpose than man or buildings are under *their* particular concepts. Yet Kant would want to say that treating human beauty or the beauty of churches without seeing men or churches *as* men or churches would lead to very odd aesthetic assessments, namely pure judgements of taste where in fact impure judgements are called for.

There is a further objection to interpretation (3). The notions of 'falling under the concept of an end' and 'representing nothing' were supposed to bring out what to disregard in nature and in art respectively when pure aesthetic appraisals are at stake: purpose or its absence is relevant to nature alone, representation or its absence to art alone. But this rigid separation does not work. For it is clear that it is not only in the context of appraising natural objects that we may have to disregard or bracket off what they are for. Even wallpapers have a function – that is of covering our walls pleasantly and appropriately – which plays no part in our assessment of them as freely beautiful. Decorative patterns have purposes as flowers or humming birds have, though in the context of human use rather than in nature's economy. The third interpretation fails to make good the claim to have found two *differentiating* criteria under the general condition of 'what an object ought to be'.

It seems to me that Kant holds this third view, at least for some of the time, and if he is not consistent, this may be because he did not distinguish it from the view which I have labelled interpretation (4). There is, in fact, direct evidence that at times he was thinking along the lines of this last interpretation. In a passage that applies equally to free beauty in nature and to free beauty in art he says: 'In the estimate of free beauty (according to mere form) we have the pure judgement of taste. No concept is here presupposed of any end for which the manifold should serve the given Object, and which the latter, therefore, should *represent* . . .' (§ 16, 229/230, my italics). Representation here must be representation *of a presumed end*, and then we seem to get something like possibility (2) where 'not falling under the concept of an end' was to be seen as an instance of 'representing nothing'. We now, therefore, have a view that can avoid the difficulties of (2) whilst bringing in the important notion of perfection, of what an object should be. Reading the quoted passage in the light not of (2) but of (4), we have to consider the possibility that 'representing nothing' and 'not falling under the concept of an end' may be jointly implied in some sense by 'presupposing no concept of what the object should be'.

Once again we have to divorce 'representation' from 'depiction'. For we now get, for nature, that things are freely beautiful when they are not, in our appraisals, bound up with the concepts of their natural ends or purposes and *therefore represent nothing*. And, conversely, when we appraise a natural object for the beauty it has *as* exemplifying its end or purpose we pass an impure judgement of taste and appraise the object as *representing* its purpose, not as just having it. Obviously 'representation' now does not mean presenting a picture or likeness of the pur-

pose or end, but embodying the end so that its possible perfection, 'what the object ought to be', shines through. If this
holds for nature it must, on reading (4), hold for art also. Although it is by no means clear that Kant consistently excludes
connotations of 'depicting' from his conception of dependent
beauty it seems at least possible to do so. (I shall try to show this
later.) Appraising a man-made object as freely beautiful would
be, as it is in the case of natural objects, appraising it with no
regard to the concept of an end under which it may or may not
fall, and *therefore* as representing nothing. Here, too, we could
remove the connotation of 'depicting' from 'representing' by
thinking of those situations in which the man-made object *could*
be seen both as under the concept of an end (wallpaper patterns
have a purpose or function *qua* wallpaper, etc.), *and* without
such ends being relevant to the appraisal, so that 'representing
nothing' would have no connection with what the pattern might
or might not depict, for example flowers or leaves. What, if anything, is depicted is irrelevant, simply because the status of
being freely beautiful can be granted solely on the grounds of
fulfilment of the general condition, namely 'not presupposing
a concept of what the object ought to be, or should be'.

In view of the advantages of relative clarity and consistency
offered by the fourth interpretation we might hope to attribute
it to Kant as his considered position. But the difficulties are still
great, and they appear with special force when we turn to his
treatment of dependent beauty in the impure judgement of
taste. The pleasing symmetry of nature and art that the fourth
interpretation seemed to establish must be put into question
again.

(III)

Dependent Beauty and the Impure Judgement of Taste. In our discussion of four views of the sort of relationship between things
in nature and products of art Kant might have had in mind, a
particular conception of how free beauty is related to dependent
beauty seemed to emerge: with respect to any object of aesthetic
appraisal it ought to be possible to make both pure and impure
judgements of taste. For whether we think of the object's beauty
as free or not free depends on our attitude towards the object,
on whether or not we disregard or keep in abeyance any idea of

the object as falling under 'final' concepts or the concept of perfection. To whatever we can ascribe dependent beauty we can
also in principle ascribe free beauty and *vice versa*. However,
Kant also says things which suggest that sometimes he took the
rather different view that some objects, whether natural or man-
made, intrinsically possess free beauty while others intrinsically
possess dependent beauty. Or perhaps we should say that some
things are intrinsically the topic of pure judgements of taste,
others of impure ones only.

This is especially clear in the case of man; but man, of course,
occupies a unique position in Kant's scheme. He both belongs
to a natural species and is a member of the 'kingdom of ends';
moreover of man only is it possible to speak of an *ideal* of perfection, an ideal therefore of dependent beauty. It would take
us too far from the topic of this paper to consider what the dis-
tinctiveness of man as a subject of aesthetic appraisals of the
impure kind exactly amounts to, but it is obvious that human
beauty does not fall easily or unambiguously into the realm of
nature, and even less into that of art. The point is relevant to a
general question that can be raised here about dependent beauty.
That is, do we, according to Kant, consider products of nature
and art for their beauty because we think of them in terms of
what they can be or ought to be, or is it rather because these
objects are already inextricably tied to teleological concepts that
when we predicate beauty of them we relate such beauty to an
idea of perfection ? On the first alternative, the notion of perfection arises because we look at something aesthetically; on the
second, certain objects – those which already stand under the
concept of perfection – force upon us a certain kind of aesthetic
appraisal, namely the kind which ascribes dependent beauty.

Now the strong emphasis Kant places on human (dependent)
beauty makes it difficult to distinguish and keep on parallel lines
those arguments that might be relevant to nature and those
relevant to art. For human beauty does not fit either category
without strain. Since men share with, say, flowers membership
of a natural order of things, it seems we ought at least to be able
to ask why what holds for one should not hold for the other. If
flowers may be the subject of pure judgements of taste when we
disregard their biological function, and hence a conception of
perfection of their kind, so it ought to be with man. It ought, in

general, to be possible in each case to disregard the conceptual framework attached to them as species or kinds. Even if there is more to man than his being of a natural kind, as is presumably not the case with flowers, the ties of each with natural ends should make for parallel treatment of them as objects of possible pure judgements of taste. Yet Kant does not think so: the ascription of beauty to man is, it seems, always an *impure* judgement of taste, thus bringing human beauty closer to the beauty of those man-made things that stand unambiguously under the concept of a purpose: buildings *qua* dwellings, *qua* churches, *qua* palaces, and so on. For in these instances our thinking of them as beautiful is tied to what they can be and must be seen *as capable of being*, that is, to an idea of their possible perfection. In this respect man has more affinities with some products of art than with natural objects: to exclude a reference in the case of the former to what they *ought* to be is to take away the grounds for ascribing beauty to them in a way which would not hold for the latter. We have then to say that the dependent beauty of at least some things follows from the fact that what these things *are* is logically connected with what they *ought to be*, rather than from the way or ways in which we may choose to regard them. The point comes out through the examples Kant selects. In a given object, he says, there may be many features which are in themselves pleasing but which detract from the object's beauty when viewed under the concept of what the thing as such ought to be. Thus, in the case of human beauty, Maori tattoos, however attractive in themselves, conflict with our conception of the dignity of man, and this must be decisive for any judgement of taste we may make. Similarly, facial features pleasing in themselves may not be congruent with what a particular kind of person is supposed to be: for example women are allowed to be pretty, warriors not. Human beauty, then, spoils any clear-cut symmetry of criteria in respect of beauty in nature and beauty in art, whether free or dependent. But it might be said that the beauty of man is after all a very special case. If we set it aside the picture may become clearer. Whether it does so or not depends on whether we can provide a solution to a problem already mentioned but not yet resolved, namely, the unclarity of the notion of representation with which Kant is working.

The examples Kant gives of dependent beauty in art are

clearly of two kinds. Sometimes they are of man-made objects that we might describe in the broadest sense as functional: churches, palaces, dwelling houses, town halls, and so on, in fact all works of architecture; and when he wants a central case of dependent beauty it is this sort of illustration on which he tends to draw – examples from art rather than from nature. Moreover, in none of *these* examples does the notion of representation as depicting appear, although it is this notion that on an orthodox reading one would have expected to underpin the contrast between free and dependent beauty. Sometimes, however, Kant does use illustrations that seem to involve the notion of representation in the narrower sense, that is, depicting or portraying something as subject matter, or suggesting in the formal composition of elements something that has real or ideal existence outside the work of art. Kant includes amongst examples of art works having a subject matter music set to words, programme music illustrating some theme or other, and perhaps we can add pictorial art that is not purely decorative but portrays people, events or situations, as well as dances with a 'story-line', plays and works of narrative literature. We do not need to enter here into familiar controversies over formalist treatments of these cases. For even if we grant to the formalist that there is a way of approaching them in terms solely of tonal, visual or verbal composition, that is regarding them for the free beauty of sound, line, rhythm, and so on, this does not seem to be what Kant recommends. Rather, he strongly suggests that these are dependently beautiful things because their beauty can be fully appreciated only when we see or hear what the formal composition suggests.

Now from the way Kant introduces his two kinds of example it seems that he thinks the criteria for ascription of dependent beauty to each are the same. But how could this be so? If we take interpretation (4) as our model we might say that functional works are beautiful because they fall within a conceptual scheme of expectations we have about what they ought to be. Their beauty, whilst no doubt residing in their formal characteristics, emerges as the beauty not just of formal composition, but of perfection (or approximation to it) of the formal arrangement of something meant to be a certain thing, representing it in the non-pictorial sense introduced earlier. The object is thus called beautiful since it yields aesthetic pleasure not despite but because of what it can be and should be seen *as*.

The second type of dependent beauty in art is more difficult to fit into interpretation (4). The narrow sense of 'representation' as 'depicting' or 'portraying' has some kind of application; yet, although works of pictorial art, music, dance or narrative literature may have conceptual connections in this way with what it is they depict, portray or suggest, it cannot be *these* conceptual connections on which their beauty is dependent. The relationships of verisimilitude and correspondence to something beyond the work do not establish a connection with the notion of what the work ought to be, in the sense in which the conceptual ties with what a building is for and can be seen *as* do. Under interpretation (4) we are trying to establish just such a connection. If, however, we take it that works of the second type do not represent, in our revised sense, because they depict, that is, what they depict is not what they represent, we could bring these cases under interpretation (4) in this way: their perfection lies in what they can be seen, heard, or experienced *as*, and only then might we say that they can be experienced as portraits, narratives, and so on. The conceptual expectations aroused by the formal arrangements in the work direct our attention not so much to what is depicted but to how the depiction is achieved. They thus represent in the wider sense – that is, not what they depict, but rather what they can be seen *as*, namely portraits, narratives, and so on. In so far as this is achieved in the disinterested experience that delights in the form in which the object represents what it can be, the work appraised is dependently beautiful.

The point to stress here is that on this interpretation considerations of form would not be reserved for the contemplation of the freely beautiful. Dependently beautiful things also would be beautiful in virtue of their form, only in their case this beauty is intrinsically linked with the concepts in terms of which we envisage 'what the things should be'. This does not mean that beauty follows from concepts: this would indeed run counter to Kant's most basic conditions for anything figuring in an aesthetic appraisal. It means rather that concepts of what something should be, rather than concepts of what an object is, can be invoked as reasons for ascribing beauty to something experienced as a building, a church, or a piece of music set to words. Within this scheme the same sorts of reason could be adduced for dependently beautiful things in art, whether we are dealing with function or with representation in the narrow sense of depiction. We could also say that dependent beauty in art *and* in nature may be picked out and distinguished by the same general criteria. For we have already seen that human beauty must be recognised not in any merely formal features but in the deep expressiveness of human potential.

It must be admitted, of course, that this interpretation attributes more to Kant than the text bears out. Certainly there is no indication that he saw that the notion of dependent beauty involves two quite different types of art objects, namely functional *and* representational in the narrow sense, so that his use of the notion of 'representation' could cover both representing purpose, end or ideal, *and* portrayal or depiction. Kant very often uses examples of a functional building and the portrayal of an object with no apparent awareness that they are not 'representational' in the same sense, and therefore not *prima facie* 'dependently beautiful' for the same reasons.

While we may have to concede that Kant wants to regard the criteria for dependent beauty in nature and in art as the same, it is by no means clear that he can actually do so in his own terms. There is a partial convergence in natural and artistic beauty when ends and purposes are considered, for example in flowers and buildings. But this leaves out art that portrays or depicts. It also raises questions about the propriety of speaking of disregarding purposes in the provision of grounds for attributions of pure rather than dependent beauty. Whilst proper and defensible in the case of flowers it seems not to be so in the case of architecture. Either, then, the conceptual ties are stronger in the case of dependent beauty in art than they are in nature – which seems improbable if we consider that nature presumably was not made for aesthetic contemplation, while this might well be an important element in the intentional structure of art – or whatever conceptual ties there are can be considered or disregarded at will, a claim which runs counter to there being two kinds of beauty at all. In either case there is no uniformity of criteria.

The conclusion we have to draw, I think, is that Kant's compressed formulations in § 16 concerning dependent beauty suffer from the same sort of unclarity and ambiguity as do his apparent assertions about the uniformity of free beauty in nature and in art. Although Kant obviously *wants* to hold (*a*) that the beauty of functional objects, for example architecture, is dependent in the same way in which the beauty of objects that portray is dependent, and (*b*) that both are dependently beautiful by the same criteria as, for example, the beauty of human beings, which belongs to nature, the evidence of the text is not strong enough definitely to attribute either of these views to him.

(IV)

I have argued in Sections II and III with respect to claim B that Kant may indeed have thought the grounds for attributing the two kinds of beauty, free and dependent, were in each case the same for nature and art, but that the text, compressed as it is, does not make a clear case for it. It is open to a number of interpretations I have sketched, none of which unambiguously accords with Kant's own formulations. His statements and examples are marred by constant conflation of the notions of purpose, end, perfection and representation. When we try to sort these out it seems we can achieve coherence only at the price of distorting or ignoring some of the things he actually says. In particular, the notion of representation remains ambivalent. Sometimes it appears that Kant could not have meant by it the depiction or portrayal of something in artistic form, although at other times it appears that this is the meaning he intended. To resolve this conflict would require an analysis of the concept of representation so that portrayal of subject matter would be only one way in which something having aesthetic form could be said to represent, whilst the central meaning would be reserved for exemplification of whatever a thing could be considered capable of being, that is, its perfection. Kant makes moves in this direction but they are not carried forward to any convincing conclusion.

Enough has been shown, nevertheless, to undermine the idea so often canvassed that Kant's aesthetic theory directly supports the view that non-representational art in the modern sense of abstract art provides the paradigms for pure judgements of taste and that, conversely, art that portrays or depicts is *for that reason alone* material merely for impure aesthetic appraisals. We have only to look at the kind of examples that Kant uses to illustrate dependent beauty. On the one hand there is architecture, where nothing is relevantly depicted or portrayed and which is yet dependently beautiful only, for the work of architecture stands under particular concepts of function or purpose without which it could not properly be appraised aesthetically. On the other hand we have programme music, portraits, narratives, and so on, where the narrower sense of 'representation' finds a place, but a subordinate one. On my suggested reading we could say of examples of the second sort that we call them dependently beautiful because it belongs to their nature, to what they could be and so ought to be, that they depict or portray. 'Representation' is then linked with the end or perfection of the object, and not with whether or not this end includes portrayal or depiction of something.

Whether we hold that Kant was simply unclear about the place of representation in his aesthetic theory, or whether we press upon him some view that attempts to bring his various statements into a particular focus, as I have tried to do, we cannot in any case enlist him in support of that notion of representation which the defenders of abstract art need in order to make a case for the primacy of non-representational over representational art. And we cannot on the basis of *that* distinction insist on the view that what figures in pure judgements of taste – free beauty – is aesthetically preferable and intrinsically more valuable than what figures in impure judgements of taste – dependent beauty. Such value judgements do not follow from Kant's analysis. Certainly they do not follow from claims A and C, which are undeniably Kant's, nor from them in conjunction with B, which, as I have argued, conceals a nest of unresolved problems.

It is interesting to note that Kant is usually appealed to when aestheticians wish to emphasise one sort of *art* (abstract) over another (representational), but rarely, if at all, in order to assess the competing claims of beautiful things in nature. The kind of aesthetic theory which would assign greater value to the beauty of flowers than to that of human beings has few followers. Yet the contrast between free and dependent beauty extends to objects of nature and ought, it seems, to result in a similar scale

of preference for them. But there is no indication that Kant sub-
scribed to such a scale, indeed his preferences seem, if anything,
to run the other way. This alone should make us wonder whether
he really did think arabesques had the edge over the Parthenon.
For in spite of the obscurities in Kant's exposition we have to
grant, I believe, that he himself thought that what held for art
with respect to free and dependent beauty held for nature also.

It is not really in question, however, whether Kant says in so
many words that pure beauty is aesthetically preferable to impure beauty, for the answer to that is simply that he does not.
The question is rather, I suppose, whether Kant's theory lends
plausibility to such preferences. Now it is true, of course, that
when Kant brings out the conceptual features of aesthetic
appraisals for which he seeks necessary presuppositions he
stresses almost *ad nauseam* the central importance of the apprehension of pure form. His question, 'What makes aesthetic
judgements possible?' turns out to be a question about *pure*
judgements of taste. No doubt the emphasis here is dictated by
Kant's conception of the nature of transcendental inquiries
as finding the presuppositions of *a priori*, non-empirical,
that is *pure*, judgements. But once a further kind of aesthetic
judgement is introduced, namely impure judgements of taste,
then, if the main inquiry is to go through, these must be brought
into some sort of relationship with pure judgements. It is in this
area that my discussion lies. Given the nature of the inquiry,
however, it can be no part of Kant's purpose to compare the two
kinds of judgement in respect of their status in a hierarchy of
values. The conclusion of his discussion of the distinction in
§ 16 is in fact completely neutral in *that* debate. To be aware of
the distinction is to realise that in many apparent disputes of
taste two people may really be at cross-purposes, because the
disputants are not disagreeing in their aesthetic judgement but
simply making different kinds of judgement. One is making a
judgement of free beauty, the other of dependent beauty, about
the same object. It cannot then be the case that the argument
could be resolved by applying general principles and deciding
automatically in favour of the pure judgement of taste, for there
is indeed no argument to resolve. We can suppose that on the
grounds on which each judgement is made neither can be
faulted if they otherwise satisfy the criteria laid down for them.

As Kant says:

> But in cases like this, although such a person should lay
> down a correct judgement of taste, since he would be esti-
> mating the object as a free beauty, he would still be found
> fault with by another who saw nothing in its beauty but a
> dependent quality (i.e. who looked to the end of the object)
> and would be accused by him of false taste, though both
> would, in their own way, be judging correctly . . . This dis-
> tinction enables us to settle many disputes about beauty on
> the part of critics; for we may show them how one side is
> dealing with free beauty, and the other with that which is
> dependent. . . . (§ 16, 231)

The impure judgement of taste is not a pure judgement
manqué. If there are in nature (man) and in art (functional art
and all art which is not purely decorative) objects about which
pure judgements are possible but out of place, that is which
would miss the very connection with the notion of ends and purposes on which dependent beauty rests, then there cannot be
any question of a preference for pure judgements over impure
judgements, free beauty over dependent beauty, non-representational art over representational art.

5

Schiller's Kant : a Chapter in the History of Creative Misunderstanding

(I)

There are many fascinating pupil-teacher relationships in the history of thought. That between Friedrich Schiller (1759–1805) and Immanuel Kant, almost entirely one-sided (Kant took little notice of Schiller), is one of the most fascinating of all. It is in essence an exemplification of that struggle to reconcile polar opposites by which Schiller's philosophy is mainly characterised. Schiller's manipulation of Kantian concepts is like nothing so much as an attempt to persuade the stylised figures on an antique vase to step down and begin living. The struggle, naturally, is prolonged and severe. It leads, in Schiller's conception of the nature and scope of aesthetics, to a whole series of misunderstandings of Kant, as well as to a number of profound and original insights into the unacknowledged aims and suppressed tendencies of Kant's own thought. I want to discuss an early stage in Schiller's encounter with Kant's philosophy during which Schiller's own venture into aesthetics first took shape. This will only lead up to and briefly touch upon the much better-known and better-documented stage of Schiller's mature aesthetic thought in the *Letters on the Aesthetic Education of Man*,[1] throughout the writing of which the struggle with Kant continued.

We think of Schiller primarily, of course, as one of the great poets and dramatists in the German language. But it would be a mistake to regard his philosophical writings, of which there are a good many, as peripheral to his achievement. Schiller himself certainly did not think so. He wrote in one of the letters to his patron, the Duke of Schleswig-Holstein-Augustenburg (9 February 1793):[2] 'It seems to me that in order to formulate a theory of art it is not sufficient to be a philosopher; one should have practised art itself, and this, I believe, gives me a certain advantage over those who will doubtlessly outstrip me in philosophical insight.' Learning by one's mistakes, he says, 'is more likely to lead to clear insight into the sanctuary of art than the safe way of never-erring genius'. In this he was quite opposed to Kant, who insisted that *his* inquiry had not been 'undertaken with a view to the formation or culture of taste (which will pursue its course in the future, as in the past, independently of such inquiries)' (*Critique of Judgement*, Preface, 170). For Schiller, but not for Kant, the theoretician had to be a practitioner, and in his writings we find a complex interplay of theory, art and life issues, which makes them often difficult to grasp. As an artist Schiller was obsessed by conflicts and contrasts, longing for their resolution and harmonisation. In his poetic and dramatic writings he excelled in the tragic genre, despite his acknowledgement of the idyllic as the highest mode of artistic achievement; in his theoretical work he often pitted one concept against another, its polar opposite, gaining from their conflict subtle modifications of them, new relationships and fresh insights. The themes of conflict and resolution were omnipresent.

Unlike Kant, Schiller was acutely aware of historical process, considered, however, from the perspective of a critic of civilisation. Schiller was in love with the idea and ideal of classical Greek antiquity from which he saw subsequent history as falling away. Consequently he was a passionate reformer, deploring his times, advising, beseeching and hectoring his contemporaries. What was required, he maintained, was a fresh awareness of the aesthetic potentialities of man as they had once been fully realised in Greece. The Greeks, Schiller believed, had in a short efflorescence produced social and political institutions that nourished instead of hampered the individual search for self-fulfilment. For Schiller a man becomes fully human through willing to be human, through consciously working at the formation of his personality. His humanity was not a natural endowment, not, as in Goethe's phrase, 'embodied form developing through living',[3] but a spiritual achievement and the end or goal to be struggled for against the temptations of easy conformity. The necessary means *and* end were art and aesthetic contemplation. 'Aesthetic education', education through and towards the aesthetic, is a key concept in Schiller's thought and a key to his personality. But mere Rousseau-like nostalgia for past attainment Schiller considered an unnecessary luxury. Attainment of the goal was for him a permanent possibility. Even if the tendencies of his time were towards fragmentation and dissociation in society, man was, he thought, never beyond hope. Wholeness, he believed, was attainable, and it was so through aesthetic education. In the psychological analysis of his own self and of the ills of his society Schiller's conception of the aesthetic stands for wholeness and integrity.

The connection of this with Kant may well seem obscure, but it is in fact fundamental. Kant's philosophy provided Schiller with a philosophical system in which polar concepts were essential ingredients and in which the dual nature of man was conceptually articulated. Kant's doctrine of faculties, or human capacities, seemed to account perfectly for the duality which Schiller felt within himself, and for himself as the type or exemplar of modern man. As a Kantian he accepted that sense and intellect, morality and reason, were distinct domains; but their separation was for him not a matter of logic but of regret – something to be overcome. He recognised that this conflict was one of the mainsprings of his creative ability and one of the targets of his analytical thought to which he returned again and again with astonishing perseverance. He lived what Kant conceptualised: the union of the sensuous and cognitive nature of man whose highest fulfilment lay in moral action. Schiller was a moralist who wrote no treatise on morality. All his thinking took the form of reflections in aesthetics, which for him was not an additional discipline to, say, ethics or epistemology but the essence of a philosophy of man: in the aesthetic sphere all partiality and incompleteness were brought to consummation, all contrast and conflict to resolution and fulfilment. In one of his letters to his friend Gottfried Körner, Schiller captured this essence:

> To be governed by the beautiful or by a feeling for art is nothing else than to have a tendency to make everything whole, to bring everything to perfection.[4]

Schiller's reading of Kant involved considerable distortion. He read him as if he were reading a diagnosis of a difficult but not hopeless case, the case of his – Schiller's – own self, and in himself that of the modern world. He cared little that Kant's concepts were not those of descriptive psychology or historical assessment. If they served these purposes, so much the better. If they proved recalcitrant, he questioned neither their soundness nor the use to which he was pressing them. Rather, he tried to improve upon Kant by extending their field of application, or by highly idiosyncratic interpretations of the conceptual moves that Kant had allowed.

The Kant that Schiller drew upon in this way was not so much the Kant of the *Critique of Judgement* but of the *Critique of Pure Reason* and the *Critique of Practical Reason*, the last providing in the end the most satisfactory approach to an aesthetic which Schiller hoped to develop. While he rebelled against what seemed to him its undue rigidity, it was Kant's moral philosophy that influenced Schiller most profoundly, though not always in a direction of which Kant would have approved. All Schiller's concepts were original adaptations of Kantian terms, often highly modified, yet carrying with them many of the Kantian associations in addition to polemical revisions of the master's ideas. What Kant punctiliously separated as logically distinct, with definite limits of application, Schiller persistently conflated. The illegitimate extension of a concept beyond its proper field became for Schiller an illuminating extension, a means towards the synthesis of partial disciplines.

Schiller often began his own investigations with a question that in the sequel turned out to be unanswerable. It is true that an answer of some kind emerges, yet usually one that shows that the question ought not to have been asked. The great value of Schiller's investigations, therefore, lies not in the questions asked, nor in the answers to them, but mainly in the critique of the questions that intrudes as Schiller's argument develops. The questions are usually Kantian in Schiller's interpretation if not in fact. Perhaps it can be said that the problematic nature of the questions is simply a consequence of Schiller's misunderstanding of Kant's philosophy, but Schiller's treatment of them is nevertheless illuminating, for it brings Kant's thought into sharper focus than do many of the commentaries of his more conventional pupils.

Schiller, it turns out, did not produce another version, however modified, of descriptive aesthetics that had culminated in Kant. He did not analyse a region of the mind, a field of investigation, which was already there to be investigated. The trend of his entire thought was directed rather towards constructing what had not been there before. Moreover, in a sense this had to be so, for whatever qualified for the attribute of 'aesthetic' in Schiller's opinion was that which is newly created, whether it be works of art or attitudes towards life or sensitive appreciation of natural and man-made configurations. Aesthetic endeavour was always directed towards achieving something, towards transposing and transmuting given conditions so that their limitations could be utilised and overcome. Theoretical speculation in aesthetics traced possibilities and projected from what was available a programme for development. In Schiller's thought theory, psychology and history came together in the conception of the aesthetic. Schiller's writings thus constitute a code that is doubly hard to crack: they employ an obsolete terminology and adhere to a system that is constantly put in question by procedure and results. What I want to do now is undertake a partial breaking of this code.

(II)

In Schiller's letters of 1793 to his friend Körner, known collectively as the *Kallias Letters*,[5] we find his first attempts to come to terms with eighteenth-century aesthetics. Here Schiller plays through the current aesthetic themes, commenting upon them and expressing his dissatisfaction with the proposals made by other philosophers. They had all, in his view, forced aesthetic questions into the mould of one or another specific philosophical position; no one, not even Kant, had succeeded in providing answers to the most elementary questions in a way that ruled out competing answers. Following the tradition Schiller regarded the question 'What is beauty?' as one such elementary question to which an answer was essential for any aesthetic inquiry to get under way. The definition he supplied and re-iterated in all the *Kallias* letters is: 'Beauty is freedom in appearance.'[6]

What is interesting about this definition is not so much what it says, which is in any case obscure, but how it is arrived at, emerging as it does from a criticism and rejection of alternative views. We get some valuable clues from a longish passage in a letter to Körner (25 January 1793)[7] in which Schiller presented what he took to be then the *status quo* in aesthetics:

> It is interesting to note that my theory is a fourth possible mode of explaining the beautiful. One can explain it either as objective or as subjective; and then either as sensuous-subjective (as with Burke and others), or as rational-subjective (as with Kant); or as rational-objective (as with Baumgarten, Mendelssohn, and the whole tribe of perfectionists [i.e. the Wolffians]), or finally as sensuous-objective – a term which will not as yet convey anything to you, though you will no doubt note its difference from the other three. Each of the preceding theories is confirmed by parts of experience, and obviously each contains part of the truth. The mistake seems to lie in the fact that each takes that part of beauty which it covers for beauty as such. The Burkean is definitely right as against the Wolffian when he maintains the immediacy of the beautiful, its independence from concepts; but he is wrong as against the Kantian when he assigns the beautiful to the merely affective sphere of sensibility. The fact that most beauties which can be experienced are not completely freely beautiful, but logically tied, falling under the concept of a purpose – as do all works of art and most beauties of nature – seems to have misled all those who see beauty as visible perfection; for here the logically good is mistaken for the beautiful. Kant wants to cut this knot by assuming a *pulchritudo vaga* and a *pulchritudo fixa*, a free and an intellectualised beauty. And he maintains, rather strangely, that beauty seen under a purpose is not pure beauty, that is to say, that an arabesque or something similar is, when considered for its beauty alone, purer than the highest beauty of man. I concede that his remarks may have the greatest merit of separating the logical from the aesthetic, yet they seem after all to miss the concept of beauty entirely. For beauty manifests itself in its supreme glory when it conquers the logical nature of its object, and how could it conquer where there is no resistance? How could it bestow its form upon a completely nondescript matter? I at least am convinced that beauty is nothing but the form of a form, and that that which is called its matter must needs be formed matter. Perfection is the form of matter, beauty on the other hand is the form of this

perfection, the latter thus standing to beauty as matter stands to form.

From this passage one might get the impression that Schiller knew what he was talking about, that is to say, that he was completely at home with the various moves of the chess pieces of eighteenth-century aesthetics. In fact, however, his description of the moves amounts to a new game with rules of doubtful coherence. Nevertheless, something of value emerges from the re-allocation and manipulation of concepts, with regard both to criticism, explicit or implicit, of Kant, and to Schiller's own proposal that beauty is 'nothing but the form of a form'.

Schiller's argument in the passage I have quoted becomes more intelligible when it is seen as formally though not materially reflecting Kant's more celebrated distinctions between the *a priori* and the *a posteriori* on the one hand, and the analytic and the synthetic on the other. Kant rejected the equation of the *a priori* with the analytic, and of the synthetic with the *a posteriori*, which he took to be implied by traditional eighteenth-century rationalism and empiricism. He recommended instead that we make a careful distinction between our mode of epistemological access to propositions (either *a priori* or *a posteriori*) and their content (either analytic or synthetic). We then get the possibility, and perhaps even the actuality, of synthetic *a priori* propositions – thus cutting across the formerly accepted dichotomy.

Schiller's intention, in analogy with these Kantian distinctions, seems to have been to set up contrasts between, on the one hand, the rational and the sensuous and, on the other, between the objective and the subjective in aesthetic theory. The rational-sensuous distinction would then seem to be comparable to the 'modal' (mode of access) distinction between the *a priori* and the *a posteriori*; and the objective-subjective distinction comparable to the content analysis of propositions into analytic or synthetic. Just as Kant denied the equation of the synthetic with the *a posteriori* in epistemology, so Schiller seemed to deny the equation of the sensuous with the subjective in aesthetics. And, similarly, as Kant denied the equation of the *a priori* with the analytic, so Schiller, in aesthetic theory, denied the equation of the rational with the objective. This line of approach might seem initially quite promising, and if Schiller had been able to

go on to give a truly Kantian analysis to support these allocations
and distinctions, the result might have been something of a
break-through in aesthetics. But this could not be, for the mean-
ings of the concepts with which Schiller was working here are
not Kantian, nor are they pre-Kantian, but a mixture of both –
or rather a slide between them, which ends in confusion.
Schiller believed that he was looking at the divisions in the
tradition of aesthetics and at Kant's own position entirely in
Kantian terms, using concepts with which he and everybody
else was familiar, in unambiguously Kantian ways. This, however, is clearly not the case. (That the analogy breaks down can
be seen if we consider what Schiller's equivalent to Kant's synthetic *a priori* is supposed to be: the sensuous-objective. In
Kant's terms this would have to be the impossible combination
of the synthetic with the analytic.)

The sensuous-subjective can, of course, be easily recognised
as the empiricist view of aesthetic experience, as exemplified for
instance in Burke; and the rational-objective is recognisably the
rationalist account, such as Baumgarten's, of aesthetic judgement as laying claim to knowledge. But *which* terms in these two
pairs are we to think of as expressing the modes of awareness or
access ? I have suggested that 'rational / sensuous' must be seen
in this role, and this seems the only way in which we can make
sense of the later parts of the passage. For Schiller agreed with
the rationalists that beauty was objective. But the rationalists
further believed that *because* beauty was objective, it was grasped
as the content of intellectual apprehension, of *rational knowledge*. Burke and the empiricists, on the other hand, thought
that beauty was 'only subjective', and as such not an object or
content of knowledge but rather something accessible to feeling,
in the sensuous mode.

There is a difficulty here concerning Schiller's use of the term
'subjective' to qualify not only sensuous awareness as in the
empiricist doctrine, but also rational understanding as in the
Kantian doctrine, according to Schiller's reading of Kant. For
this, on the face of it, is to reduce the classification to absurdity.
To think of beauty as 'merely subjective' makes good sense when
this view is associated with sensuous awareness, as in the empiricist approach; but it is extremely difficult to see how beauty,
thought of as subjective, could be rationally apprehended or

understood. Yet this is the view Schiller attributed to Kant. In Schiller's opinion Kant had rightly tried to retain what was valid in the two conflicting doctrines of empiricist and rationalist aesthetics; but he had gone astray in retaining the empiricists' merely *subjective* status of beauty instead of the sensuous awareness of it. Consequently, Kant according to Schiller was reduced to a kind of rational insight into something whose nature was essentially subjective.

So far as the subjective/objective distinction goes, Schiller, we might say, marginally preferred the rationalist approach to aesthetic phenomena – as objective contents of knowledge – to the empiricists' view. But he certainly did not wish to couple the objectivity of beauty with rational cognition of it as Baumgarten did. Kant at least had seen that this was untenable. Baumgarten, whose position Schiller knew well, is indeed typically represented as holding that aesthetic cognition is a mode of knowledge, although in some respects he was closer to Schiller than this suggests. For Baumgarten the characteristic *perceptio confusa* of aesthetic perception was the perception of things as wholes. This is not analytical, like the higher cognitive processes of the understanding, but neither does it, like the inferior faculties of sensuous awareness or practical orientation, treat its contents merely as pointers to purposes beyond themselves. Rather, this in-between mode of Baumgarten constitutes awareness of things in *con-fusion*, fused together, in such a way that their beauty is recognised and enjoyed as an objective property of wholes.

What Schiller objected to in Baumgarten was exactly this in-between status of the aesthetic mode that made it an inferior form of rational understanding. Schiller did insist on the objectivity of the content of an aesthetic experience, but the experience, he thought, had to be uniquely itself, not to be contrasted favourably or unfavourably with any other form of awareness or apprehension. Kant's investigations, therefore, were particularly promising, for Kant too saw aesthetic experience as *sui generis*. In analysing it however, Kant, Schiller thought, had got his logical wires crossed. He had settled for subjectivity, not objectivity; for rational understanding, not sensuous awareness.

Schiller is here less than just to Kant, but the discontent is

symptomatic of a real difficulty in Kant that others also have
felt. Kant, in Schiller's view, had argued in the following way:
Baumgarten had mistaken 'the beautiful for the logically good',
that is to say, he had thought of the beautiful as that which is
perfect of its kind. Correctly recognising that this was a mistake,
Kant had then wrongly drawn the conclusion that beauty had
nothing to do with perfection of an instance of a kind. But
realising that this would not quite do either, he had further
supposed that there were after all two kinds of beauty, free and
adherent, only the first of which could be properly described as
purely aesthetic. For adherent or dependent beauty belongs to
the perfection of things manifesting purposes, and these fall
under the concepts of the understanding. But if pure aesthetic
beauty does not fall under concepts at all, the ideal of beauty for
Kant, as Schiller interpreted him, was the empty arabesque,
whether Kant desired this or not.

   Now of course if we had to stand by this interpretation of
Kant's doctrine of two kinds of beauty we might feel non-
conformist misgivings.[8] But can we in any case accept Schiller's
diagnosis of where Kant went wrong when this is essentially
bound up with the ingenious conceptual scheme underpinning
Schiller's own proposals? According to Schiller, Kant's root
mistake was an overhasty acceptance of Burke's idea that beauty
is *subjective*, so that *what* was experienced as beautiful had to be
free of purposiveness, for purposiveness, Schiller believed,
would have to imply *objectivity*. If, however, we thought in
Schiller's own terms of the sensuous but rational we could think
of that which was objectively beautiful as *not* concept-free, so
long as its conceptualised nature could be sensuously experienced, not merely rationally analysed. The intelligibility of
Schiller's own alternative, therefore, stands or falls with his
criticism of Kant's alleged root mistake about the subjectivity
of beauty. But was it a mistake?

   Assuming, as Kant – and Schiller at least at this early stage –
did assume, that aesthetics is the science of the beautiful, Kant
saw the investigation as one into the *mode in which* beauty is
experienced. His aesthetic, therefore, is essentially a theory
about the kind of experience from which judgements upon the
beautiful, or judgements of taste, issue. Following the British
thinkers Kant had then linked aesthetic experience to sensuous

pleasure, thus avoiding a kind of conceptualisation which yet eludes the understanding. He also maintained, however, that judgements of taste demanded universal assent because of some – and to Schiller obscure – feature of rationality in the experience that guaranteed the application of aesthetic concepts. This questionable linkage of the intersubjective validity of judgements of taste with sensuous pleasure was unnecessary, Schiller argued: all that was required was to recognise that beauty was objective and yet distinguishable from perfection of kind or purpose. The attempts of Kant and Burke to account for the 'immediacy of beauty' drew attention away from the essential inquiry: they provided a phenomenology of aesthetic experience in which the 'object' becomes simply any x that satisfies the experience described. Whereas what we needed, Schiller thought, was a definition of beauty, and only secondarily and consequentially an analysis of aesthetic experience. We should then see that beauty was objective, yet appearing to the imaginative capacities of man: beauty is 'sensuous-objective'.

Schiller's argument here depends on attributing to Kant the view that 'beauty itself' is subjective, whereas for Kant, of course, to speak of beauty as subjective could only be to refer to our subjective experience of it. No sense could otherwise be attached to speaking of *beauty* as subjective. Moreover, the reason in Kant's view for expecting universal assent to judgements of taste, in spite of the individuality of the aesthetic experience, is the necessary requirement or presupposition of all such experiences, namely, that they have a structural similarity and so are in that respect shareable experiences. Aesthetic judgements, however, remain subjective for Kant in the vital sense that they concern objects only in so far as they elicit from the judging person or subject a confirmation of his humanity in the harmonisation and balanced activity of all his powers and capacities. If this was Kant's view, however, his insistence that it is the *object* that is beautiful fits together uneasily with the overriding emphasis on aesthetic enjoyment as the successful integration of the subject's experiences, for which the object seems at best a catalyst.

Had Schiller made *this* point he would have been right, but this was apparently not foremost in his mind when he described Kant's theory as subjective. 'Subjective' for Schiller was in problematic contrast to 'objective' to which he assigned an entirely un-Kantian significance, a manoeuvre which is obscured by his assumption that his vocabulary was Kant's. The meaning of 'objective' for Schiller in fact reached back beyond Kant to the ontological sense of 'independently real', or 'real in itself', to be set against, or opposed to, 'subjective'. But, of course, in Kant's philosophy the notion of the subjective and the objective are not opposed but complementary: the experience of beauty is that of an experiencing subject who, through his experience, in some sense 'constitutes' the object of his experience. In insisting that the experience of beauty was 'sensuous', therefore, Schiller could equally well have said that it was 'subjective' in any sense important to Kant.

He *could* have said that, that is to say, had he not, contrary to what he supposed, used the term 'sensuous' in both a Kantian and an un-Kantian sense. In Kant's epistemology the term 'sensuous' is ascribable roughly to those items that belong to the empiricists' parsimonious basis of sense experience. It refers to what is given in sense-awareness without the structuring of categories, and thus certainly not to anything objective. For Kant, therefore, to speak of the 'sensuous-objective' must be meaningless. Schiller's own use of the term 'sensuous' was, by contrast, much richer, coming closer to what in Kant's scheme was covered by the ambivalent and, I believe, basically obscure doctrine of the productive imagination. When Schiller spoke of the empiricists' 'sensuous-subjectivist' view he unwittingly adopted the narrower Kantian sense, as for example when he said of the followers of Burke that they assigned the beautiful to 'the merely affective sphere of sensibility'. The result is a slide from the richer sense to the less rich, which obscures Schiller's whole attack on the empiricists and on Kant. If the criticism of Kant is conducted in terms of the richer sense of the term 'sensuous', it becomes inexplicable why Kant was accused of replacing it with a reference to the rational element in aesthetic experience, for this richer sense could accommodate what Kant wanted, although he himself would not have used this term. If the criticism of the empiricists is conducted in terms of the less rich sense, it is difficult to see why Schiller's own use of 'sensuous' to describe *his* position is not open to the same objection he levelled against Kant and the followers of Burke.

It is clear then that Schiller's application of the phrase 'sensuous-objective' does not make sense in the Kantian scheme and cannot therefore count as improving on Kant. Indeed, the pair of concepts it is supposed to replace in Kant's aesthetics, namely, 'rational-subjective', is not truly Kantian either. For to describe Kant's position as rational-subjective in contrast to Baumgarten's, which is rational-objective, and to do so in criticism of Kant, seems to attribute to Kant a view that he expressly denied: that the recognition of beauty is a matter of reason or understanding. But why should such an attribution be made? Schiller's overhaul of Kant's system was, obviously, a restructuring of it. This, however, was after all inevitable if we remember what Schiller's purpose was. He wanted, he said, to supply Kant with an 'analytic of beauty' which was lacking in Kant's own system. Yet this entailed an account of beauty as 'objective' in a sense completely alien to Kant.

(III)

It might well be said that in trying to disentangle the efforts of a well-meaning, self-confessed philosophical amateur we could not in any case hope to gain any illumination of Kant. But I have suggested that Schiller's arguments, whatever their intrinsic merits or demerits, locate areas of difficulty for many readers of Kant. One of these is the problematic distinction already mentioned between free and dependent beauty. The apparent primacy of *pulchritudo vaga* over *pulchritudo fixa* arises, as Schiller correctly saw, as a consequence of the need to separate 'the logical from the aesthetic'. The kind of beauty which attaches to things perfect in their kind, dependent beauty, is logically tied to our conception of what sort of thing it is; the other kind, free beauty, belongs to a formal configuration independently of the nature of the sort of thing it is. The dilemma for Schiller, to whom this kind of formalism was deeply repugnant, was how then to reconcile the elements of the two kinds of beauty without sacrificing Kant's insight into the uniqueness and independence of aesthetic experience, and without relapsing into the rationalists' equation of beauty with perfection as grasped by the intellect. Schiller's solution was that we should think of the beautiful as that which 'appears in sense awareness'.

For if we conceived of beauty in this way then we would not simply *identify* it with the perfection of things thought of in terms of concepts and purposes. Only when the perfection of things *appeared* to us in sensuous awareness would their beauty become manifest. Moreover, its appearing in this way would still leave a clear sense in which beauty was *objectively* manifest, not a private creation. It would be what he called in the passage I quoted from the letter to Körner the 'form of a form', that is the appearance to the senses of intelligible perfection. Beautiful things would be experienced as beautiful when the form that really belonged to them, perfectly adequate to their matter, appeared to the beholder as 'form of a form'.

Although we might by now have some comprehension of how Schiller's views emerged from his complex misuse of Kantian terms, it is still obscure how his frequently repeated definition of beauty as 'freedom in appearance' is to be derived from this development – in particular, how this definition becomes associated with the demand for objectivity. This requires a wider view of Schiller's understanding, appreciation and criticism of Kant, for it involves a particular reading on Schiller's part of Kant's moral philosophy.

Condensing a complex view into a sentence, we can say that the applicability of the concept of freedom guarantees for Kant that man, who is himself a being amongst other beings in the world of natural phenomena, is also a citizen of the kingdom of ends, and that man's moral striving is not subject to the limitations imposed on the world of his cognitive experience. The series of contrasts that arise here between the concept of freedom and nature, between the moral and natural law, and between the moral agent and 'natural' man, are logically based; and so is the contrast between phenomena and things-in-themselves that underpins them in Kant's philosophy. It is not then a matter for regret that the concept of freedom is not to be found among, or associated with, the concepts of the understanding, nor is it deplorable that we cannot know things-in-themselves. It would be nonsense to speak as though we ought to be able to. Nevertheless, Kant himself thought of the contrasts in terms of gaps to be bridged, at least when he supposed that the third Critique was such a bridge. Whatever we make of this supposition in Kant's philosophy, it is this that Schiller chose to see as the central problem to which aesthetics can provide a solution. Kant's third Critique suggested to Schiller a way of reconciling freedom with appearance.

Taking note of Kant's epistemological veto on penetrating the 'veil of appearances', Schiller saw, or thought he saw, that the veil had nevertheless been penetrated in Kant's ethics. What was not imprisoned within man's limited understanding, but freely acknowledged by the will, had to be 'objective' in the sense he had been trying to make room for. Now if we could think of the concept of freedom as applicable not merely to moral agency but also to sensuous delight then we could say that such experiences were not subject to the limitations of the concepts and forms of understanding. We could speak of our experiences of beauty as experiences of the real freely appearing. This definition, moreover, fitted Schiller's specifications: beauty, objective and real, is manifest to sensuous appreciation; that is it is sensuous-objective.

Schiller could achieve this result only, of course, by rejecting some basic features of Kant's philosophy. Paradoxically, the authority of Kant is cited in defence of a view which, if it is to be at all intelligible, implies that Kant was fundamentally mistaken. But any plausibility that Schiller's theory has seems to rest on echoes of Kantian concepts. Through the various metamorphoses that the term 'appearance' undergoes in Kant *and* Schiller the idea that it concerns what is given to sense persists. But whereas what, for Kant, is given to sense is given only within the framework of the categories and space and time – the principal theme of the first Critique – Schiller's view implies a rejection of this. For Schiller 'appearing' is the shining forth of things and configurations that are free in the sense of not falling within this framework, and it is things as so appearing that he calls 'beautiful'.

Schiller, to be fair, was aware that what 'appeared' in Kant's sense was never independently real. The divergence from Kant is, nevertheless, nowhere more clearly evident than in his struggle to make an objection against Kant in a language still ostensibly Kantian. One might think of Schiller's definition of beauty as either a deplorable conceptual muddle or an admirable *tour de force* giving new or metaphorical significance to the characteristic doctrines of transcendental idealism. (In much the same way we might think of Hegel's 'sensuous presence of the idea', which has a similar source in the third Critique, namely in Kant's remark that the beautiful is symbolic of the good.) However derived, the new definition of beauty, Schiller confided to Körner, provided the basis for an 'analytic' of beauty such as Kant himself had not supplied. This 'analytic' Schiller never elaborated in any detail and, indeed, although the definition reappears from time to time in slightly different guises, it is never again offered as satisfying the requirements of the 'sensuous-objective' demand. The protracted struggle with Kant had, it seems, set Schiller free to put aside what, at the beginning of his aesthetic thought, he regarded as his primary task: to define beauty. Schiller never admitted that it was a mistake to try for a definition, nor did he ever suggest that his definition might be defective. 'Beauty is freedom in appearance' remained in Schiller's later writings not as something to be argued for or proved, but as something to be applied and in order as it was. We cannot, however, on this account ignore the informal discussions of the *Kallias Briefe* when we turn to his published writings on aesthetic themes.

These letters form the background to the roughly contemporaneous essay *On Grace and Dignity*.[9] We do not find here any tortured or tortuous juggling with the concepts of 'beauty' or 'goodness' or 'freedom'. Instead of a typology of concepts or an analytic of beauty we get what might be described as an analytic of human nature, a characteristic arrangement of thought about two ideas that are the hybrid offspring of aesthetics and ethics. The influence of Kant is strong, but Schiller now seems to take for granted the possibility of fusing Kantian epistemology with Kantian ethics. Grace and dignity are, Schiller claimed, freely beautiful and beautifully free phenomena, not exactly phenomena in the Kantian sense, but so called with Kant in mind. The unselfconscious balance of graceful behaviour and the conscious mastery of adversity in dignified action, whatever other significance they may have in human behaviour, can be contemplated *as if* they were things of beauty. In selecting just these concepts of grace and dignity for special treatment Schiller provided examples of his bridging operation in action. But this was not all: he was also pointing to a feature of Kant's moral philosophy that Schiller rejected, namely, the separation of acting morally from acting from inclination. To withhold approval from *all* actions done from natural inclination rather than from duty, to attach no value to action freely undertaken and without constraint, seemed to Schiller a gross aberration. He therefore returned to Shaftesbury's idea of 'moral grace' and to what he himself called the *'schöne Seele'* ('beautiful soul'), which has the capacity to act morally as second nature – an eighteenth-century ideal of decorum and fittingness elevated to a moral accomplishment. This was not a notion that Kant's moral philosophy could accommodate although Schiller was inclined to think that it should.

Schiller established the alleged Kantian pedigree of his two concepts with characteristic panache. To begin with, acting with dignity and with grace are polar notions, as are Kant's conceptions of acting from duty and acting from natural inclination. But whilst Kant was prepared to see aesthetic value in grace, he certainly did not find it in duty, whatever we are to make of the problematic distinction between the sublime and the beautiful. As a master of tragedy, of course, Schiller was bound to treat Kant's notion of the sublimity of adherence to the moral law with profound respect. But equally, as a writer of tragedies, he demonstrated again and again what theoreticians since Aristotle have known, namely that the tragic *dénouement* does not destroy but miraculously enhances our capacity to respond to its beauty. In Schiller's language, when sublime dignity is made artistically apparent the result can be experienced as beautiful. The practice of the theatre alone therefore throws doubt, in Schiller's view, on Kant's separation of the beautiful and the sublime with its implied contrast between the aesthetic and the moral. But the separation is also theoretically groundless. Schiller tried to show this in his treatment of 'grace' and 'dignity'. For though they are polar concepts, representative of the aesthetic and the moral, they characteristically generate a polemical point against Kant. Exploiting a useful ambiguity, Schiller found grace and dignity when properly understood not mutually exclusive but complementary. They are manifestations of the fully active and morally engaged person, manifestations as they *appear* – and this, for Schiller, indicated their aesthetic character. In the end the notion of dignity deriving from Kant's conception of the sublime loses its Kantian status as a specifically moral concept.

Moral achievement through being experienced acquires an aesthetic dimension, an aspect of beauty. It 'appears' gracefully.

Schiller did not begin by openly acknowledging this apparent reversal of the roles of the sublime and the beautiful. He did so later in a kind of postscript to the essay on grace and dignity, the *Tabulae Votivae*,[10] no doubt with the prodding of his co-author Goethe. Here the reversal is explicit:

> If you cannot live beautifully,
> It is yet left to you reasonably to will,
> To do as a spirit what, as a man, is denied to you.

The ideal is a beautiful humanity. We may, or some of us may, have to be content with less, yet even then we can act with dignity: pure morality is still possible when beauty of soul has not been achieved. Schiller had profound respect for those who, feeling the constraint of the moral law, obey its demands, but he thought that only they are *constrained* to obey whose free consent has not been given. Dignity can be saved from pomposity or moral complacency when it is not made the end of human behaviour but is achieved almost inadvertently under great stress. We *respect* what is dignified because the impossible has been attempted; we *love* the morally beautiful because here the apparently impossible has become manifest.

In these early chapters of Schiller's thought, then, we have the foundations for his mature thought expressed in the *Letters on the Aesthetic Education of Man*. 'Freedom in appearance' there becomes transposed into the key notion – Schiller's own, though with constant glances over the shoulder to Kant – of aesthetic semblance. Things in their natural state or persons in their moral actions appear to the senses as beautiful; freedom in appearance is the attribute of anything which either is or is *as if* alive. Contrary to what many suppose, this is not a mere aesthetisation of the world of morals and nature. The split felt in human nature is healed in the aesthetic sphere where man's moral and natural inclinations legitimise each other. To live and experience aesthetically is to have moral freedom; but to exercise this freedom we must know the extent of our aesthetic capacities. Schiller was gradually approaching his formulation in the *Aesthetic Letters* of the aesthetic as free play, totally untrivial and yet totally free. 'Man plays only when he is fully human, and he is only fully human when he plays.'[11]

What I have been trying to do is to bring out something of Schiller's debt to Kant. From the point of view of the professional philosopher Schiller's complex distortions and misunderstandings of his mentor are deplorable. Yet I believe this is a chapter in *creative* misunderstanding, leading eventually to one of the most fruitful theories in aesthetics. A few years later than the discussions I have been talking about Schiller announced in a famous distich that he had eventually shaken himself free of Kant:

> Two decades you cost me: ten years I lost
>
> Trying to comprehend you, and ten to rid myself of you.[12]

Perhaps, however, the price was not too high.

6

The 'As-If' Element in Aesthetic Thought

(I)

The attempt to understand the peculiar status of things that stand out from our world of theoretical and practical concerns – the constructions of art – leads to the recognition of the notion of fiction. As parts of this world works of art are man-made things, apparent statements or gestures, and formal configurations. When we consider what they are they baffle us in their gratuitousness on the one hand, and by their claim to our full attention on the other. What they say, do, or present affects our lives; we would be less complete without them. Yet they are not strictly necessary to our living. From the very beginnings of thought about art this has been acknowledged: in rejecting art as false, as pretence, as deception; in justifying art as imitation; in glorifying art as pure appearance. What remains is the recognition of a situation in which what we have come to mean by 'fiction' is exemplified. From the things we have in art, from the configurations artists have made and are making, we are led to see a contrast: that between things we use and things which use us; that between statements whose value we can cash out in the exchange of information and description and statements whose value enriches us without purchasing power; that between what is true or false, however complicated, and what is neither true nor false, however illuminating; that between the straightforward and the oblique; that between what is real and what is artificial.

We consider art in many different ways and in a variety of contexts. Even when we are not explicitly concerned with its status, discussion of art proceeds against the background of what we take for granted about art. It is my thesis that in aesthetic discourse the recognition of the subject matter – art – provides a model of construction and fictional procedure and determines the manipulation of the concepts we use to talk about it. I wish further to maintain that aesthetic discourse is not 'aesthetic' by virtue of special concepts employed in it, but by virtue of the constructive use we make of concepts, and I am going to call this the aesthetic use of concepts. In general this tends to the recommendation to use the term 'aesthetic' adverbially rather than in an adjectival fashion: we consider things aesthetically; we use concepts aesthetically; we proceed aesthetically.

Using concepts aesthetically is to use them in some relation and with some kind of reference to the things and situations of art and in general to what we might call 'aesthetic objects'. Aesthetic discourse about art accepts implicitly that what it deals with is fictional; it accepts that we are dealing with constructions and devices, with things which look *as if* they were something or other, with statements which read *as if* they were saying or asserting something, with configurations which appear *as if* their conjunction made a point. To think aesthetically is to think about those fictions. But it is not the same as thinking fictively; this general point had better be briefly discussed first.

What art exemplifies thinking can repeat: the mode of artificiality, the obliqueness of constructions without counterparts. Thought structures themselves can be fictive and follow artistic model situations in respect of procedure. We can think *as if* something were the case, although it need not and often cannot be shown to be so. This is an important ingredient in theoretical conjecturing. On many occasions we can and have to proceed as art does, by trying out fictions in our theoretical proposals. This does not mean that such thinking and art are indistinguishable. In thinking fictively we follow a mode in which art presents itself. In art we have as-if things and as-if assertions – to no further purpose. Fictive thinking is procedure by construction of often unconfirmable, or as yet unconfirmed, hypotheses, and this is always done for definite purposes, as for instance in operating with specific theories for the solution of particular sets of problems. Art itself provides models for such procedure. But it has to be approached not by fictive thought but by thought that recognises the fictive nature of that with which it deals. To think and to speak aesthetically is to be aware of and articulate about the nature of some things as fictions. It is to conceive of things in a special kind of bracket—the 'as-if'.

Aesthetic discourse, as I shall argue in some detail later, is committed from the outset to the task of transposition, transposition of concepts used and developed for the purposes of non-aesthetic discourse – for example discourse about things and actions and problems – into the key of aesthetic usage.[1] For concepts in aesthetic discourse are used to talk about what is not straightforward, about that which deliberately presents an appearance. Terms functioning in such discourse are terms aesthetically transposed into the key of 'as-if' expectations. I do not propose this as a novel discovery. I believe aesthetic transposition to have been practised in all worthwhile discussion of art. But it has not often been clearly recognised for what it is. Awareness of what is involved can help, I believe, to avoid some errors and confusions that inevitably arise when transposed statements are read as untransposed, when legitimate obliqueness is handled with illegitimate literalness, when wrong expectations are brought to bear on aesthetic discourse.

A wide range of concepts can function aesthetically under certain conditions. The conditions are those of reference to aesthetic objects, and they can be summarised, though not enumerated, as the requirements of as-if situations. This amounts to a denial of the view that what makes discourse aesthetic is the employment in it of specifically aesthetic concepts. In any case the range of concepts that could perhaps qualify as native to the aesthetic sphere is exceedingly small; they consist mainly of derivatives and qualifications or negations of 'beautiful' and its closest associates. To be restricted to this range would not only make for a poverty-stricken aesthetic vocabulary; it would also suggest commitment to a unique and mysterious faculty of taste. Instead, I wish to suggest that concepts with which we are perfectly familiar in other contexts can be used aesthetically. A sphere of reference is then established that alters the ordinary function of such concepts and transposes them. Transposed concepts need a kind of handling that does justice both to their function in transposition and to what they establish on this new level.

Aesthetic discourse constructs conceptual frameworks in which to discuss what is itself the outcome of novel construction in art. In art fictions are given, artistic statements are in the fictional mode, and we know this by the contrast they present to what is ordinarily and straightforwardly the case. But what is it, then, that these works appear to be and seem to say? Almost all theories that have asked such questions as to what art works are, do, or mean have come up with answers, however reluctantly, to the effect that works of art appear to be for their own sake and mean only themselves.

Such statements are often regarded with suspicion and considered to be unnecessarily far-fetched and esoteric. But it seems to me that this is, after all, the best way there is to describe what works of art are. Saying that they are 'for their own sake' and 'mean only themselves' *is* to recognise their as-if character, their fictional nature. For this is just what things ordinarily and statements normally *are not*. Things and statements are in relation to this or that, about this or that, referring to or explaining this or that. Things normally never are just 'for their own sake'; statements never mean 'just themselves'. When we consider them in this way, as we do on occasion, we consider them aesthetically. This requires special circumstances for detachment, for being able to stand back. Or it requires works of art: things which are 'in their own right', 'for their own sake'. This is what artists have constructed for us – appearances of self-sufficiency, apparent microcosms.

This is why I speak of a key into which concepts are transposed when we use them aesthetically. To be an object of aesthetic discourse is to be considered for its own sake. But there is no terminology for something 'in its own right' since we do not normally find things 'for their own sake'. We – or artists – construct such things. In our ways of speaking about them we accept this by transposing our language about ordinary things and states of affairs into a language about things that appear to be just for themselves. The 'as-if-in-its-own-right' is what every art work more or less successfully proclaims – more or less, for the achievement can be partial, tentative, or even missed, as we all know. We understand the aesthetic situation because we live in a world in which it is possible to speak *as if* something were the case. One might even say that this is possible because there are and have been works of art – but I shall not press this point. Works of art appeal to our capacity for as-if transposition. In this respect the view that understanding and appreciation of art is itself re-creative seems unobjectionable.

Objects of aesthetic discourse, whilst not amenable as such to straightforward discussion in terms available for non-aesthetic thinking, can nevertheless be discussed in terms largely borrowed from ordinary contexts and made to function with reference not to ordinary things but to things that are so constructed that they stand alone, as if in their own right. For this we need no uniquely aesthetic vocabulary, only a uniquely aesthetic use of whatever vocabulary comes to hand. We talk about works of art in whatever way is at our disposal from other contexts – from contexts of things in relation, of things as means, of actions for purposes, of statements as informative and descriptive – and then relate such terms anew to the art work in its constructed isolation. Thus our language is constantly being specified as we go along, with the work or the group of works or the aesthetic situation supplying the centre of reference to which particular statements become relevant when they highlight the constructional character of what is being discussed. Showing relevance is to make terms derived from, say, history, biography, iconology, biology, sociology, and so on, operate in a new context so that the object becomes amenable for discussion as an aesthetic object.

This entails what has often been denied: that there is nothing that can be known from other contexts that is as such irrelevant to an aesthetic discussion. What is irrelevant can only be decided for particular cases, not legislated about in advance. Aesthetics may be 'autonomous'; but this cannot mean that non-aesthetic information is irrelevant to it. There is no aesthetic information as such. What we know and what we have got has to be made relevant to the constructions we have before us. In aesthetic discourse we talk obliquely, as every art work itself does. To say things indirectly, by presenting an appearance, is a principle not only of irony but of art. To describe art works and to state something about our reactions to them is to make sense of the seemingly gratuitous, artificial contrivance of 'things in their own right'. Transposing descriptive terms from the level of description of things for this or that purpose to that of things as fictional constructs is usually achieved by building in the as-if factor, which is rarely announced explicitly. It can be shown, however, to be operative in critical and evaluative discussion of art works in which features that are recognisable as features of things and statements are discussed as features of presented microcosms. Lines, colours, sounds, shapes, words, stories, episodes, scenes, movements, masses, and so on, are ingredients in art works on which we may concentrate with all the knowledge we have from other contexts. Aesthetic use is made of this when it serves not to describe things, but to disclose that such things construct and enclose their own world of reference.

(II)

The figure of Kant looms in the background of any discussion of the principles of aesthetic discourse. His philosophy seems highly relevant to a view that emphasises a mode of as-if thinking – even when one does not go as far as I have done in suggesting a mode of as-if existence for art works themselves. One is immediately reminded of Kant's view that a pure judgement of taste does not employ objectively determinate concepts but only 'indeterminate' ones that postulate the possibility of inter-subjective agreement without our being able to appeal to the normal guidelines of validity. Such judgements, according to Kant, are judgements in which all cognitive faculties operate in harmony and balance, in 'free play', as Kant was fond of calling it. The play terminology, so prominent even in Kant's most abstract arguments, is significant: it adds up to an implicit recognition of the as-if element in aesthetic thought.[2]

Kant's problem was to find a theoretical formulation for the apparent subjectivity of aesthetic judgements, and the equally undeniable fact that aesthetic judgements appear to be of the same propositional structure as theoretical and practical judgements and yet do the work of neither. Kant's analyses often begin by asking questions in terms of different kinds of judgements, concentrating on the function of differently orientated concepts; but they usually end by attempting to explain the differences of conceptual functioning in terms of the differences in origin and habitat of concepts, that is by reference to faculties of experience. I believe that this is an unnecessary step in many of Kant's discussions, and that the force and usefulness of his transcendental arguments can be preserved without invoking the highly artificial distinctions of reason, understanding, sensibility, or imagination: that is, without appeal to a structure of mentality. The important arguments in Kant's Critical philosophy remain unimpaired by this. The arguments from experience as we have it to the presuppositions of our having it can be restated without loss as arguments from a given complex situation to a theory in which such a situation is amenable to explanation. What often makes access to Kant so difficult nowadays is his outmoded and philosophically suspect language of 'faculties of experience', and this is particularly prominent in his analyses of aesthetic experience in the third Critique. What Kant describes as the harmonious interplay of all our faculties in the aesthetic mode could be less ambiguously characterised as the transposition of descriptive statements into the aesthetic key. This would be preferable because it bypasses the need to defend a unique capacity for aesthetic awareness which, when denied (as is logically and psychologically possible), leaves aesthetic concepts without a point of reference. To postulate a faculty of taste or a special capacity for the awareness of beauty has, in all theories that have been driven to this, led to variously disguised forms of circular argument. If taste is the awareness of aesthetic qualities in things, and aesthetic qualities in things are features discovered by taste and formulated in taste concepts, then the circle is vicious. It can be avoided at the cost merely of giving up the view that there are peculiarly aesthetic properties or qualities, and substituting instead an account of the aesthetic use of concepts in which terms descriptive of property features are transposed to meet the requirements of aesthetic discourse.

To speak of the Kantian 'as-if' is to raise the spectre of Vaihinger. Kant was the acknowledged inspiration for his *Philosophy of 'As If'*.[3] But from a sound insight into the indirect value of fictive constructs, Vaihinger was led to fictionalise all worthwhile thinking that could promote conceptual advance. This excess might seem to make the raising of Vaihinger's spectre unprofitable and the laying of his ghost unnecessary. Yet the suggestiveness of the details of some of his analyses remains, and anybody using the as-if terminology at all disregards the work of Vaihinger to his loss. Vaihinger paid his debt to Kant by interpreting some of Kant's tentative suggestions on the heuristic value of fictions so that they read like a coherent systematic view – which, of course, they were not. The essence of Kant's as-if concepts, as Vaihinger interpreted them, is that they are concepts that we choose to employ in an effort to bring intelligible order into a given subject matter despite the fact that we do not expect to find objective counterparts to such conceptual structures. The justification for using them is that they are found on the whole to work. Vaihinger devoted a large part of his book to an investigation of Kant's work in order to document the fictive method without so much as mentioning the Critique of Aesthetic Judgement. Yet here, if anywhere, one would have thought, Kant is making proposals to consider the content of experience in an as-if fashion.

For Kant the aesthetic situation to be explained is that of our being able to make judgements and assessments that do not fall within the range of cognitive-scientific or practical-ethical judgements and that are yet judgements, that is, propositions stating something, although their validity cannot be checked by objective criteria. The fact to be explained, as Kant sometimes put it, is that judgements of taste claim to be irrefutable and are yet unenforceable.[4] In so far as they are incapable of proof they behave *as if* they were merely subjective; and in so far as they nevertheless claim universal validity they behave *as if* they were objective.

When Kant speaks of 'purposiveness' in nature and art, and especially when he adds 'without purpose' for the aesthetic context, he draws attention to configurations that appear patterned in conformity of parts, functions, and elements without our being able to say what the pattern is *for*, except that it seems to be for our enjoyment. He appeals to situations that appear suited to our capacity to enjoy ourselves. 'Purposiveness without purpose' is how Kant describes what we seem to find. It may be seen as the basic as-if proposal underlying his explanation of the peculiar structure of aesthetic judgements. According to Kant we approach objects aesthetically when we recognise with delight, wonder, and arrested attention the structural patterns of things; when, despite being unable to say *that* they exhibit purpose, we approach them *as if* they did. Only by refusing to go beyond the 'purposiveness *without* purpose' can we, according to Kant, sustain the authentically aesthetic response. Kant's autonomy of the aesthetic refers to the independence of aesthetic contexts from theoretical concern with finding causes and

explanations and from practical concern with utility and sub-
servience to ends. Kant's aesthetic realm is autonomous in that
it exhibits the possibility of harmony without explanation and
finds this possibility confirmed by an experience that proceeds
as if purposiveness were achieved and obvious.

But judgements based on the assumption of purposiveness or
finality can never be shown to possess what Kant calls 'objective
validity'. For all that can validly be asserted about matters of
fact is what is amenable to description in terms of objects within
the categorial scheme; and all that can legitimately be demanded
and prescribed about human situations is what is available for
moral injunction on the basis of the moral law. Kant's fundamental distinction is always that between thought which is
related to data and mere thought; the latter is possible, and even
has its own rules, but it can never claim objective validity. In the
Dialectics of all three Critiques it is Kant's contention that
ignoring such a distinction leads to metaphysical and logical
illusion. In terms of the Kantian system the field of objectivity –
either objective knowledge or legitimate prescription for action –
is therefore exhausted by understanding and reason, and
exhaustively covered by the *Critique of Pure Reason* and the
Critique of Practical Reason respectively. In terms not based on
the Kantian system – although, I believe, not in un-Kantian
terms – this means that what we can know are things and events
in the space-time world, and what we can practically legislate
for and legitimately praise and blame are human actions in a
context, including those of the solitary individual whose deci-
sions, however dependent on his own assessment of the moral
law, are moral only when the universalisability of the maxims at
stake brings in a reference to other individuals. Even without
commitment to Kant's doctrine of understanding as providing
constitutive principles for knowledge of objects, and of reason
as providing insight into morally binding precepts, one could
say that factual and moral statements are assertions of what is or
ought to be the case. What is given is always in a context, which
makes it possible to formulate individual statements so that they
can be checked for correctness against the background of that
which, and of that in terms of which, they assert. In Kant's
system this means that cognitive-scientific judgements can have
objective validity because the structure of understanding

(faculty of rules) and of reason (faculty of postulation) guarantees this. Ordinary theoretical and practical judgements employ concepts suitable for things in a system and actions in a scheme: concepts to cope with what we meet as in this or that context.

Kant saw that judgements of taste lack this link with either a system of rules or a scheme of postulations. He concluded that therefore such judgements do not have objective validity, but subjective validity only.[5] Much of his Critique of Aesthetic Judgement is an elaborate attempt to establish that these subjective judgements nevertheless have some kind of necessity. One might say that what Kant calls 'objectively valid' statements belong to discourse employing concepts on the expectation that something conforms to them and is expressible by means of them; and what he calls 'subjectively valid' statements belong to discourse employing concepts on as-if assumptions, that is to say, employing concepts derived from contexts where they are adequate for description or prescription, and using them *as if* they were adequate to the things we discuss aesthetically.

Kant puts it that judgements of taste are therefore without determinate concepts; sometimes he even says that ascriptions of beauty and cognate judgements are judgements without concepts. This seems to me better captured (and to do more justice to the facts of the richness and variety of aesthetic discourse as we find it) if we deny not that aesthetic discourse makes use of concepts, but that it makes exclusive use of specifically aesthetic concepts. Kant comes very close to this when, speaking of 'indeterminate' concepts, he suggests an 'indeterminate use' of them. If we think of situations where concepts that in other contexts are used 'determinately' now function 'indeterminately', we have the Kantian model for aesthetic transposition. Descriptive and prescriptive concepts (for Kant the concepts of theoretical and practical judgements) function aesthetically, or are transposed into the aesthetic key, when they are used on as-if assumptions. In Kant's terminology I could say: when they are used *as if* something objectively corresponded to them while we know that it does not. Going beyond Kant I would wish to say: when they are taken from discourse about things in systems and actions for ends in order now to function in discourse about things that appear to be in their own right and actions that appear to be performed for their own sake.

(III)

So far I have thought it best not to interrupt the general course
of the argument by detailed references to those passages in the
text of the third Critique that seem to me most relevant to its
support. I shall now mention some of them.

In § 45 Kant states: 'Nature proved beautiful when it wore the
appearance of art; and art can only be termed beautiful, where
we are conscious of its being art, while yet it has the appearance
of nature.' (306). Here Kant's aesthetic key term 'beautiful'
indicates the fundamental requirement for an aesthetic object:
that it must present an appearance. Natural objects must appear
as if wrought by art, art objects *as if* produced by nature; yet in
both cases we know that this is only an appearance: 'Fine art
must be clothed *with the aspect* of nature, although we recognise
it to be art.' (307).

Fine art, according to Kant, is 'fine' in contrast to mere
contrivance (Kant here uses the older sense of 'art' which covers
anything well done), when it presents us with products and
creations; when something is given and stated with finality and
yet has no other end than itself. Kant puts this point with
characteristic reference to mental faculties in § 44: 'Fine art . . .
is a mode of representation which is intrinsically final, and which,
although devoid of an end, has the effect of advancing the culture
of the mental powers in the interests of social communication.'
(306). 'A mode of representation' suggests Kant's recognition
of the status of an art work as a fiction. For if its existence is that
of a representation it cannot be that of a thing. And it is not even
itself a representation: a 'mode of representation' is what Kant
says. I have referred to this when I described the status of art
works as that of 'as-if things'. In the phrase 'intrinsically final
although devoid of an end', Kant stresses again the necessary
appearance of purposiveness although no purpose in the strict
sense can be specified. That Kant adds a remark on the aesthetic
effect of the work does not mean that this effect on 'mental
powers' is a kind of disguised purpose. It is in the aesthetic
effect that we recognise the apparent purposiveness of things
which have been constructed – *as if* for the sole purpose of
making the balanced play of all our capacities possible. Kant's
hint at the 'interests of social communication' summarises what

he has gone through at greater length elsewhere: that the subjective judgement of taste presupposes communicability even
though it cannot claim consent or approval by appeal to the
operation of rules or precepts.

In the discussion of imagination and of aesthetic ideas (as for
instance in § 49) Kant comes closest to an explicit statement of
the fictional status of aesthetic objects. Imagination, called a
'faculty' by Kant,[6] is a 'productive faculty of cognition', not on
a level with sensibility, understanding or reason. It is to be
regarded as a mode of conjoint functioning of all mental
capacities, thus being the only fully creative aspect of mind
which Kant allows. And it is not creative *ex nihilo*: 'The imagination . . . is a powerful agent for creating, as it were, a second
nature out of the material supplied to it by actual nature.' But
the important passage in § 49 is this: 'Such representations of
the imagination may be termed *ideas*. This is partly because they
at least strain after something lying out beyond the confines of
experience, and so seek to approximate to a presentation of
rational concepts [i.e. intellectual ideas], thus giving to these
concepts the semblance of an objective reality.' (314). This
'semblance of an objective reality' is, I would say, what makes a
thing a fiction and compels us to use concepts which are taken
from the context of ordinary things in a way which now takes
note of the semblance character of constructs. This is done by
making a thing-language do the work for things in their own
right – things that are the semblances that art provides by and
for imaginative construction.

The heading of § 58 in the Dialectic of Aesthetic Judgement
may be seen as a summary of the main point I wish to emphasise.
It runs: '*The idealism of the finality alike of nature and of art, as
the unique principle of the aesthetic judgement.*' Kant is here once
more concerned with the apparent ambiguities of a principle of
taste. He has already rejected both the assimilation of aesthetic
pleasure to mere agreeableness and the obliteration of the distinction between aesthetic and moral judgements. The former
would be empiricism in a critique of taste; the latter, rationalism.
The thesis and antithesis of the two standpoints together form
the antinomy of taste which Kant – in line with his handling of
the theoretical and practical antinomies in the other two
Critiques – dissolves by showing that both are false. His own

solution is more akin to a modified rationalism than to a purely sensationalist position, which he completely discards. Now a rational principle of taste 'may take the form either of the *realism* of finality or of its *idealism*' (347), that is to say, subjective finality can be experienced either as an actual end of nature or of art, or 'it is only a supervening final harmony with the needs of our faculty of judgement in its relation to nature' (and art). Although 'the beautiful forms displayed in the organic world all plead eloquently on the side of the realism of the aesthetic finality of nature' (347), this has to be rejected, 'for in such an estimate the question does not turn on what nature is, or even on what it is for us in the way of an end, but on how we receive it' (350). Restating this we might say that aesthetic discourse only apparently describes ordinary things – apparently, because the concepts of ordinary descriptive discourse may function in it; but they function differently through underlining and highlighting a new construction that is imaginatively entertained as only for itself (Kant refers to this as 'how we receive it').

Kant concludes § 58 with these words: 'The *idealism* of the finality in estimating the beautiful in nature and in art is the only hypothesis upon which a Critique can explain the possibility of a judgement of taste that demands *a priori* validity for every one (yet without basing the finality represented in the Object upon concepts).' I would read this as supporting the view that by the fictive mode of concepts aesthetically used we can account for aesthetic discourse being about things that appear 'final', as if in their own right.

Lastly, there is Kant's formulation of the antinomy of taste (§ 56):

> *Thesis.* The judgement of taste is not based upon concepts; for, if it were, it would be open to dispute (decision by means of proofs).
>
> *Antithesis.* The judgement of taste is based on concepts; for otherwise, despite diversity of judgement, there could be no room even for contention in the matter (a claim to the necessary agreement of others with this judgement). (338/9)

Kant dissolves this antinomy by showing that judgements of taste can be taken both as based on concepts and as not based on determinate concepts. One could reformulate Kant's point as follows. Judging aesthetically we have to use concepts *as if* they referred to objects of sense; but no schematic correspondences can be exhibited for them. Yet they are not 'empty' in the Kantian sense. For their indeterminate use specifies at the same time our delight, approval, dislike or aversion *as if* private subjectivity were all that mattered. But, since we offer judgements of taste as relevant to others who see the same objects, such feelings are not 'blind' sensations either. This is the Kantian As-If of aesthetics: aesthetic judgements proceed *as if* the concepts used in them had objective validity and *as if* they described merely private feelings.

I shall end by putting this Kantian point for my own view thus: aesthetic discourse uses any concepts available from other contexts for the description of objects, transposing them so that they function *as if* the objects had left all possible context behind and were in their own right. When such objects are constructed artefacts, this is just what the artistic statement achieves: the semblance of self-sufficiency. Aesthetic discourse reflects this in its own structure. Kant's 'as if merely private' could then be taken as a pointer to the aesthetic use of discourse relying not so much on a ready-made faculty of taste in the individual who is using and constructing it, but on sensitiveness to fictions, on readiness to accept a construct both in personal experience and in thought about it, and on the capacity for sustaining an illusion.

This would have been too much for Kant. But perhaps we should say: too little. Kant himself suggested some much more extravagant directions for further thought. Because concepts are used but no knowledge is gained, and because subjective states are described but universal consent is in principle presupposed, both the objective and the subjective as-if of judgements of taste for Kant contain a reference to the supersensible. In 'purposiveness without purpose' Kant had a principle for which no object in nature can be found, through which no objective knowledge can be gained. That he should therefore conclude that it leads us to the supersensible can only be regretted; but the fact must be admitted. Similarly, the subjective side of the puzzle was seen by Kant as a strong hint of the supersensible coming through: in conceiving purposiveness that cannot be proved to be real, mind becomes aware of its own powers, of its capacity to transcend nature and to reach something beyond. This seems to me an unwarranted step to take from the arguments he provides in the formulation of the problem. Yet for Kant it apparently was a natural step, since it gave him the desired bracket by which forcibly to hold his Critical opus together. This was, after all, what he confessed to have written the third Critique for: to bridge a gap. It is for these conclusions that the Kant of the third Critique has become known, accepted, or rejected. One should, of course, know them. Accepting them means having to accept also the Kantian Critical philosophy as a metaphysical system. Rejecting them not only leaves the fruitful implications of the Kantian As-If for aesthetics; it also has the advantage of holding out some hope for an interpretation of Kant that takes the contribution of the third Critique seriously for the assessment of the other two Critiques – but a third Critique without this last step to a seemingly triumphant disclosure of the supersensible.

Notes and References

CHAPTER ONE

1. For an interesting discussion of Hume and Kant on imagination see P. F. Strawson 'Imagination and Perception' in *Experience and Theory*, ed. L. Foster and J. W. Swanson (London: Duckworth 1970) pp.31-54.
2. Martin Heidegger *Kant and the Problem of Metaphysics*, trans. J. S. Churchill (Bloomington: Indiana University Press 1962) especially § 31.

CHAPTER TWO

1. John Kemp *The Philosophy of Kant* (London: Oxford University Press 1968) p.107.
2. Lewis White Beck '*Kritische Bemerkung zur vermeintlichen Apriorität der Geschmacksurteile*' in *Bewusst Sein – Gerhard Funke zu eigen* (Bonn: Bouvier 1975) pp.369-72.
3. Norman Kemp Smith *A Commentary to Kant's 'Critique of Pure Reason'* (London: Macmillan 1918) pp.288-9.
4. See also 'Imagination and Knowledge', p.14 above.
5. Immanuel Kant *Logic*, trans. R. Hartman and W. Schwarz (New York: Bobbs-Merrill 1974) pp.119-20. In the passage quoted I have used my own translation of § 40, A 176-7.
6. op. cit., p.288.
7. Jonathan Bennett *Kant's Analytic* (Cambridge: Cambridge University Press 1966) pp.132-3.
8. W. H. Walsh *Kant's Criticism of Metaphysics* (Edinburgh: Edinburgh University Press 1975) p.92.
9. Stephan Körner *Kant* (Harmondsworth: Penguin Books 1955) pp.48-50.
10. P. F. Strawson *The Bounds of Sense* (London: Methuen 1966) Part Two, 11 'Objectivity and Unity', and pp.100-2 in particular.
11. op. cit., pp.91-6.
12. See also 'Aesthetic Appraisals', p.58f below.
13. See also pp.20-1 above.

CHAPTER THREE

1. See 'Epistemological Claims and Judgements of Taste' pp.26-31 above.

2. See 'Imagination and Knowledge', pp.5-6 above.

3. See 'Epistemological Claims and Judgements of Taste', pp.43-52 above.

4. Robert L. Zimmermann 'Kant: The Aesthetic Judgement' in *Kant*, ed. Robert Paul Wolff (London: Macmillan 1968) p.388.

5. Gilbert Ryle *The Concept of Mind*, 1949 (Harmondsworth: Penguin Books 1963) p.244.

6. See also 'Imagination and Knowledge', p.15f above.

7. See e.g. F. N. Sibley 'Aesthetic and Nonaesthetic' *Philosophical Review* LXXIV (1965) 135-59; I. Hungerland 'Once Again, Aesthetic and Non-Aesthetic' *Journal of Aesthetics and Art Criticism* 26 (1968) 421-50.

CHAPTER FOUR

1. Clive Bell, *Art*, 1915, 2nd edition 1948 (New York: Capricorn Books 1958) p.27.

2. See also pp.50-1, 56 above and 127 below.

CHAPTER FIVE

1. *Über die Ästhetische Erziehung des Menschen – in einer Reihe von Briefen*. First published in instalments in Schiller's journal *Horen*, then revised by Schiller for publication as part of his collected prose works in 1801. The best available text (English and German facing) is *On the Aesthetic Education of Man – in a Series of Letters*, edited and translated by E. M. Wilkerson and L. A. Willoughby (Oxford: Clarendon Press 1967).

2. *Schillers Briefe*, ed. Fritz Jonas in 7 vols. (Stuttgart: Deutsche Verlags-Anstalt 1892-6) vol. 3, pp.248-9.

3. '*Geprägte Form, die lebend sich entwickelt*', from *Urworte – Orphisch*.

4. 30 March 1789. Jonas, op. cit., vol. 2, p.268.

5. Schiller planned but did not complete a treatise on beauty, *Kallias*; his letters to Körner from January to March 1793 contain extensive drafts and give a very full record of his thoughts on the topic.

6. For example, letter to Körner of 8 February 1793, Jonas, op. cit., vol. 3, p.246: '*Schönheit also ist nichts anders, als Freiheit in der Erscheinung*'. See also letters to Körner of 18, 23, 28 February and 5 May 1793.

7. Jonas, op. cit., vol. 3, pp.237-9.

8. See 'Free and Dependent Beauty', pp.78-98 above.

9. *Über Anmut und Würde*, first published in *Neue Thalia* of 1793.

10. Published in *Muselalmanach* of 1797: *Die Moralische Kraft. Kannst du nicht schön empfinden, dir bleibt doch, vernünftig zu wollen,/Und als ein Geist zu tun, was du als Mensch nicht vermagst.*

11. Fifteenth Letter *On the Aesthetic Education of Man*: '. . . der Mensch spielt nur, wo er in voller Bedeutung des Worts Mensch ist, und er ist nur da ganz Mensch, wo er spielt.'

12. *Zwei Jahrzehnte kostest du mir: zehn Jahre verlor ich/Dich zu begreifen, und zehn, mich zu befreien von dir.* Written for *Xenien* of

1796, published 1893; quoted by Wilkerson and Willoughby, op. cit., p.xli.

CHAPTER SIX

1. For 'aesthetic transposition' see also my *Prelude to Aesthetics* (London: Allen & Unwin 1968) pp.9-19.
2. For a more critical discussion of 'free play', see 'Aesthetic Appraisals' pp.66-70 above.
3. Hans Vaihinger, *The Philosophy of 'As If'*, trans. by C. K. Ogden (London: Routledge & Kegan Paul 1935). I have critically explored some of Vaihinger's ideas in 'The Kantian Thing-in-Itself as a Philosophical Fiction' *The Philosophical Quarterly* 16 (1966) 233-43.
4. See also pp.70-77 above.
5. For detailed discussion of objective and subjective validity of judgements, see 'Epistemological Claims and Judgements of Taste', pp.18-52 above.
6. For comment on Kant's faculty language in this context, see 'Imagination and Knowledge', pp.5-7, 12 above.

Acknowledgements

The publisher makes grateful acknowledgement to: the Editor of *Philosophical Forum* for permission to use a revised version of 'Kant on Imagination' (vol. 11, 1971, 430–45) to form the basis of chapter 1 of this volume; the Editors of *Kant-Studien* for permission to reprint with alterations 'Kant on Aesthetic Appraisals' (vol. 64, 1973, 431–49) and 'Free and Dependent Beauty' (Akten des 4. Internationalen Kant-Kongresses, Teil 1, 1974, 247–62) as chapters 3 and 4 of this volume; the Editor of *The British Journal of Aesthetics* for permission to use part of 'Friedrich Schiller: Adventures of a Kantian' (vol. 4, 1964, 348–62) in a revised form for chapter 5 of this volume; the Editor of The Aristotelian Society for permission to reprint 'The Kantian "As-If" and its Relevance for Aesthetics' (*Proceedings of the Aristotelian Society*, vol. LXV, 1965, 219–34, © 1964 *The Aristotelian Society*) as chapter 6 of this volume. In this last, only minor changes have been made, and they include changing the Kant quotations to the Meredith translation of the *Critique of Judgement* in order to conform to quotations as used in the book throughout.

Index

aesthetic appraisals (*see also* 'aesthetic judgements' and 'judgements of taste'): absence of knowledge claims, 56, 73; aesthetic and non-aesthetic properties, 74, 75; cognitive judgements and, 55-6, 69-70; conceptual features of, 53, 54, 55, 63-70; conceptualisation and, 57, 58, 63-70, 109; cultural milieu and, 61; existence of object and, 60-2, 69; faculties of the mind and, 65, 66, 67, 69, 70, 123-5; feeling of delight and, 57-8, 59, 60, 60-3, 65, 68-9; feelings of pleasure and displeasure, 57-8, 59, 60-1, 65, 68-9, 71; general validity, 63-70; imagination and, 57, 67, 68, 69, 124-5, 129; interest and, 61-2; objects of, 56-7, 60-2, 69; perceptual acts, 57, 58, 60; presuppositions of, 53, 54, 55, 67-8, 76-7; sensations and feelings, 56-7, 58-9; sensuous gratification and, 60-1; special characteristics of, 53; subjective validity of, 63-7, 71, 76, 125; subjectivity of, 53, 55-62, 76, 77, 109, 123, 130; the agreeable and, 58, 59, 60; transcendental inquiry into, 53, 59, 67-8; understanding and, 66, 67, 68, 69, 73, 75; universal assent, 53, 54, 63-4, 67-70, 71, 76, 77, 105, 125, 131
aesthetic discourse: ideas in, 129-30; indeterminate concepts in, 127, 130-1; objects of, 122, 128; use of concepts in, 119, 120-1, 122-3, 130-1
aesthetic judgements (*see also* 'aesthetic appraisals' and 'judgements of taste'): absence of criteria of truth, 25; absence of general principles, 27; aesthetic ascription and, 27-9; as *a priori*, 18-19; 'emergent' qualities of objects, 28, 29; imagination as basis of, 3, 4; knowledge claims and, 23-5, 26, 27, 30, 56, 63; subjective validity of, 24-5, 26-9, 43, 48, 49, 51
aesthetic transposition, 120, 121-3, 127
apperception, transcendental unity of, 12, 13
a priori: /*a posteriori* contrast in judgements, 21-2, 25, 105, 106; judgements of taste and the, 18-26
art: and representation, 78-9, 84, 85, 88-9, 90, 92, 95-6; 'as if' assertions in, 119-20; concept of, 61; fiction and the understanding of, 118, 120-1, 128; purposiveness in, 125-6, 128
'as if': assertions in art, 119-20; element in aesthetic thought, 118-32; transposition, 121-3; Vaihinger's interpretation, 124-5

Baumgarten, A. G., 104, 106, 107, 108, 111
beauty: and representation, 78-9, 84, 85, 89, 90, 92, 95-6; archi-